ALL ABOUT JESUS

ALL ABOUT JESUS

Compiled by Peter Potter

Published by
William Mulvey Inc.
72 Park Street
New Canaan, Conn. 06840

Cover design: Ted Palmer

Library of Congress Cataloging-in-Publication Data

All About Jesus
"A Bull's-eye Book"

1. Jesus Christ—Meditations. 2. Jesus Christ—Words.
I. Potter, Peter (date).

BT199.A55 1988 232 86-43160

ISBN 0–934791–07–4

All Scriptural quotations are from the
King James Version of the Bible.
ABS 1967 KJ053–C Series-D–2

Printed in the United States of America
First Edition

Dedicated to the Clergy.
Men and Women who give their lives
so we can better know Jesus Christ.

Contents

PART I

THE STORY OF JESUS

Now the birth of Jesus Christ was on this wise: When as his mother Mary was espoused to Joseph, before they came together, she was found with child of the Holy Ghost. Then Joseph her husband, being a just man, and not willing to make her a public example, was minded to put her away privily.

But while he thought on these things, behold, the angel of the Lord appeared unto him in a dream, saying, Joseph, thou son of David, fear not to take unto thee Mary thy wife: for that which is conceived in her is of the Holy Ghost. And she shall bring forth a son, and thou shalt call his name Jesus: for he shall save his people from their sins.

Now all this was done, that it might be fulfilled which was spoken of the Lord by the prophet, saying, Behold, a virgin shall be with child, and shall bring forth a son, and they shall call his name Immanuel, which being interpreted is, God with us.

Matthew 1:18-23

And in the sixth month [from the conception of John the Baptist by Elizabeth] the angel Gabriel was sent from God unto a city of Galilee, named Nazareth, to a virgin espoused to a man whose name was Joseph, of the house of David; and the virgin's name was Mary.

And the angel came in unto her, and said, Hail, thou that art highly favored, the Lord is with thee: blessed art thou among women. . . . Fear not, Mary: for thou hast found favor with God. And, behold, thou shalt conceive in thy womb, and bring forth a son, and shalt call his name Jesus.

Then said Mary unto the angel, How shall this be, seeing I know not a man? And the angel answered and said unto her, The Holy Ghost shall come upon thee, and the power of the Highest shall overshadow thee: therefore also that holy thing which shall be born of thee shall be called the Son of God. . . . And Mary said, Behold the handmaid of the Lord; be it unto me according to thy word. And the angel departed from her.

Luke 1:26-28, 30, 31, 34, 35, 38

Then Joseph being raised from sleep did as the angel of the Lord had bidden him, and took unto him his wife: and knew her not till she had brought forth her firstborn son: and he called his name Jesus.

Matthew 1:24, 25

And she brought forth her firstborn son, and wrapped him in swaddling clothes, and laid him in a manger; because there was no room for them in the inn.

Luke 2:7

And there were in the same country shepherds abiding in the field, keeping watch over their flock by night. And, lo, the angel of the Lord came upon them, . . . and said unto them, Fear not: for, behold, I bring you good tidings of great joy, which shall be to all people. For unto you is born this day in the city of David a Saviour, which is Christ the Lord.

And this shall be a sign unto you; Ye shall find the babe wrapped in swaddling clothes, lying in a manger. And suddenly there was with the angel a multitude of the heavenly host praising God, and saying, Glory to God in the highest, and on earth peace, good will toward men.

Luke 2:8-14

And when eight days were accomplished for the circumcising of the child, his name was called Jesus, which was so named of the angel before he was conceived in the womb.

Luke 2:21

Now when Jesus was born in Bethlehem of Judea in the days of Herod the king, behold, there came wise men from the east to Jerusalem, saying, Where is he that is born King of the Jews? for we have seen his star in the east, and are come to worship him.

Matthew 2:1, 2

When Herod the king had heard these things, he was troubled, . . . And when he had gathered all the chief priests and scribes of the people together, he demanded of them where Christ should be born.

And they said unto him, In Bethlehem of Judea: for thus it is written by the prophet, And thou Bethlehem, in the land of Judah, art not the least among the princes of Judah: for out of thee shall come a Governor, that shall rule my people Israel.

Matthew 2:3-6

Then Herod, when he had privily called the wise men, . . . sent them to Bethlehem, and said, Go and search diligently for the young child; and when ye have found him, bring me word again, that I may come and worship him also. When they had heard the king, they departed; and, lo, the star. . . went before them, till it came and stood over where the young child was.

And when they were come into the house, they saw the young child with Mary his mother, and fell down, and worshipped him: and when they had opened their treasures, they presented unto him gifts; gold, and frankincense, and myrrh. And being warned of God in a dream that they should not return to Herod, they departed into their own country another way.

Matthew 2:7-9, 11, 12

And when they were departed, behold, the angel of the Lord appeareth to Joseph in a dream, saying, Arise, and take the young child and his mother, and flee into Egypt, and be thou there until I bring thee word: for Herod will seek the young child to destroy him.

When he arose, he took the young child and his mother by night, and departed into Egypt: and was there until the death of Herod: that it might be fulfilled which was spoken of the Lord by the prophet, saying, Out of Egypt have I called my son.

Matthew 2:13-15

And he [Joseph on his return from Egypt] came and dwelt in a city called Nazareth: that it might be fulfilled which was spoken by the prophets, He shall be called a Nazarene.

Matthew 2:23

And the child grew, and waxed strong in spirit, filled with wisdom; and the grace of God was upon him.

Luke 2:40

The Spirit of the Lord is upon me, because he hath anointed me to preach the gospel to the poor; he hath sent me to heal the brokenhearted, to preach deliverance to the captives, and recovering of sight to the blind.

Luke 4:18

Then cometh Jesus from Galilee to Jordan unto John, to be baptized of him. . . . And Jesus, when he was baptized, went up straightway out of the water: . . . and lo a voice from heaven, saying, This is my beloved Son, in whom I am well pleased.

Matthew 3:13, 17

The next day John seeth Jesus coming unto him, and saith, Behold the Lamb of God, which taketh away the sin of the world! This is he of whom I said, After me cometh a man which is preferred before me; . . . And John bare record, saying, I saw the Spirit descending from heaven like a dove, and it abode upon him. . . . and looking upon Jesus as he walked, he saith, Behold the Lamb of God!

John 1:29, 30, 32, 36

The devil taketh him [Jesus] up into an exceeding high mountain, and showeth him all the kingdoms of the world, and the glory of them; and saith unto him, All these things will I give thee, if thou wilt fall down and worship me.

Then saith Jesus unto him, Get thee hence, Satan: for it is written, Thou shalt worship the Lord thy God, and him only shalt thou serve. Then the devil leaveth him, and, behold, angels came and ministered unto him.

Matthew 4:8-11

Now when John had heard in the prison the works of Christ, he sent two of his disciples, and said unto him, Art thou he that should come, or do we look for another?

Jesus answered and said unto them, Go and show John again those things which ye do hear and see: the blind receive their sight, and the lame walk, the lepers are cleansed, and the deaf hear, the dead are raised up, and the poor have the gospel preached to them.

Matthew 11:2-5

And he cometh to Bethsaida; and they bring a blind man unto him, and besought him to touch him. And he took the blind man by the hand, and led him out of the town; and when he had spit on his eyes, and put his hands upon him, he asked him if he saw aught.

And he looked up, and said, I see men as trees, walking. After that he put his hands again upon his eyes, and made him look up; and he was restored, and saw every man clearly.

Mark 8:22-25

Then again called they the man that was blind, and said unto him, Give God the praise: we know that this man is a sinner. He answered and said, Whether he be a sinner or no, I know not: one thing I know, that, whereas I was blind, now I see. . . . he hath opened mine eyes. . . .

Since the world began was it not heard that any man opened the eyes of one that was born blind. If this man were not of God, he could do nothing. . . .

And Jesus said, For judgment I am come into this world, that they which see not might see; and that they which see might be made blind.

John 9:24, 25, 30, 32, 33, 39

The foxes have holes, and the birds of the air have nests; but the Son of man hath not where to lay his head.

Matthew 8:20

When he [Jesus] was entered into a ship, his disciples followed him. And, behold, there arose a great tempest in the sea, ... but he was asleep. And his disciples came to him, and awoke him, saying, Lord, save us: we perish.

And he saith unto them, Why are ye fearful, O ye of little faith? Then he arose, and rebuked the winds and the sea; and there was a great calm. But the men marveled, saying, What manner of man is this, that even the winds and the sea obey him!

Matthew 8:23-27

As they went out, behold, they brought to him a dumb man possessed with a devil. And when the devil was cast out, the dumb spake: and the multitudes marveled, saying, It was never so seen in Israel. But the Pharisees said, He casteth out devils through the prince of the devils.

Matthew 9:32-34

And it came to pass, as Jesus sat at meat in the house, behold, many publicans and sinners came and sat down with him and his disciples. And when the Pharisees saw it, they said unto his disciples, Why eateth your master with publicans and sinners?

But when Jesus heard that, he said unto them, They that be whole need not a physician, but they that are sick. . . . I am not come to call the righteous, but sinners to repentance.

Matthew 9:10 13

Whosoever therefore shall confess me before men, him will I confess also before my Father which is in heaven. But whosoever shall deny me before men, him will I also deny before my Father which is in heaven.

Matthew 10:32, 33

And it came to pass, that when Jesus. . .was come into his own country, he taught them in their synagogue, insomuch that they were astonished, and said, Whence hath this man this wisdom, and these mighty works?

Is not this the carpenter's son? is not his mother called Mary? and his brethren, James, and Joses, and Simon, and Judas? And his sisters, are they not all with us? Whence then hath this man all these things?

And they were offended in him. But Jesus said unto them, A prophet is not without honor, save in his own country, and in his own house.

Matthew 13:53-57

When it was evening, his disciples came to him, saying, This is a desert place . . . send the multitude away, that they may go into the villages, and buy themselves victuals.

But Jesus said unto them, They need not depart; give ye them to eat. And they say unto him, We have here but five loaves, and two fishes. He said, Bring them hither to me. And he commanded the multitude to sit down on the grass, and took the five loaves, . . . to his disciples, and the disciples to the multitude.

And they did all eat, and were filled: and they took up of the fragments that remained twelve baskets full. And they that had eaten were about five thousand men, beside women and children.

Matthew 14:15-21

Straightway Jesus constrained his disciples to get into a ship, and to go before him unto the other side. . . . And in the fourth watch of the night Jesus went unto them, walking on the sea.

And when the disciples saw him walking on the sea, they were troubled, saying, It is a spirit; and they cried out for fear. But straightway Jesus spake unto them, saying, Be of good cheer; it is I; be not afraid.

And Peter answered him and said, Lord, if it be thou, bid me come unto thee on the water. And he said, Come. And when Peter was come down out of the ship, he walked on the water, to go to Jesus. But when he saw the wind boisterous, he was afraid; and beginning to sink, he cried, saying, Lord, save me.

And immediately Jesus stretched forth his hand, and caught him, and said unto him, O thou of little faith, wherefore didst thou doubt? And when they were come into the ship, the wind ceased.

Matthew 14:22, 25-32

Then came to Jesus scribes and Pharisees. . .saying, Why do thy disciples transgress the tradition of the elders? for they wash not their hands when they eat bread.

But he answered and said unto them,. . . Not that which goeth into the mouth defileth a man; but that which cometh out of the mouth, this defileth a man. . . . those things which proceed out of the mouth come forth from the heart; and they defile the man. For out of the heart proceed evil thoughts, murders, adulteries, fornications, thefts, false witness, blasphemies; these are the things which defile a man: but to eat with unwashen hands defileth not a man.

Matthew 15:1-3, 11, 18-20

And Jesus going up to Jerusalem took the twelve disciples apart in the way, and said unto them, Behold, we go up to Jerusalem; and the Son of man shall be betrayed unto the chief priests and unto the scribes, and they shall condemn him to death, and shall deliver him to the Gentiles to mock, and to scourge, and to crucify him: and the third day he shall rise again.

Matthew 20:17-19

Many shall come in my name, saying, I am Christ; and shall deceive many. . . . If any man shall say unto you, Lo, here is Christ, or there; believe it not. For there shall arise false Christs, and false prophets, and shall show great signs and wonders; insomuch that, if it were possible, they shall deceive the very elect.

Matthew 24: 5, 23, 24

When the Son of man shall come in his glory, . . . and before him shall be gathered all nations: and he shall separate them one from another, as a shepherd divideth his sheep from the goats; and he shall set the sheep on his right hand, but the goats on the left.

Then shall the King say unto them on his right hand, Come, ye blessed of my Father, inherit the kingdom prepared for you from the foundation of the world: for I was ahungered, and ye gave me meat: I was thirsty, and ye gave me drink: I was a stranger, and ye took me in: naked, and ye clothed me: I was sick, and ye visited me: I was in prison, and ye came unto me.

Matthew 25:31-36

Then gathered the chief priests and the Pharisees a council, and said, What do we? for this man doeth many miracles.

And one of them, named Caiaphas, being the high priest that same year, said unto them, Ye know nothing at all, nor consider that it is expedient for us, that one man should die for the people, and that the whole nation perish not. . . . he prophesied that Jesus should die for that nation; and not for that nation only, but that also he should gather together in one the children of God that were scattered abroad. Then from that day forth they took counsel together for to put him to death.

John 11:47, 49-53

Pilate saith unto them, What shall I do then with Jesus which is called Christ? They all say unto him, Let him be crucified. . . .

When Pilate saw that he could prevail nothing, but that rather a tumult was made, he took water, and washed his hands before the multitude, saying, I am innocent of the blood of this just person: see ye to it. Then answered all the people, and said, His blood be on us, and on our children. Then. . . when he had scourged Jesus, he delivered him to be crucified.

Matthew 27:22, 24-26

And when they had platted a crown of thorns, they put it upon his head, and a reed in his right hand: and they bowed the knee before him, and mocked him, saying, Hail, King of the Jews!

And when they were come unto a place called Golgotha, that is to say, a place of a skull, . . . they crucified him, and parted his garments, casting lots. . . . and set up over his head his accusation written, This is Jesus the King of the Jews.

Matthew 27:29, 33, 35, 37

Now from the sixth hour there was darkness over all the land unto the ninth hour. And about the ninth hour Jesus cried with a loud voice, saying, Eli, Eli, lama sabachthani? that is to say, My God, my God, why has thou forsaken me?. . . Jesus, when he had cried again with a loud voice, yielded up the ghost.

Matthew 27:45, 46, 50

And after this Joseph of Arimathea, being a disciple of Jesus, but secretly for fear of the Jews, besought Pilate that he might take away the body of Jesus: and Pilate gave him leave. He came therefore, and took the body of Jesus. And there came also Nicodemus. . . .

Then took they the body of Jesus, and wound it in linen clothes with the spices, as the manner of the Jews is to bury. Now in the place where he was crucified there was a garden; and in the garden a new sepulchre, wherein was never man yet laid. There laid they Jesus.

John 19:38-42

The first day of the week cometh Mary Magdalene early, when it was yet dark, unto the sepulchre, and seeth the stone taken away from the sepulchre. . . . and as she wept, she stooped down, and looked into the sepulchre, and seeth two angels in white sitting, the one at the head, and the other at the feet, where the body of Jesus had lain.

And they say unto her, Woman, why weepest thou? She saith unto them, Because they have taken away my Lord, and I know not where they have laid him. And when she had thus said, she turned herself back, and saw Jesus standing, and knew not that it was Jesus.

Jesus saith unto her, Woman, why weepest thou? whom seekest thou? She, supposing him to be the gardener, saith unto him, Sir, if thou have borne him hence, tell me where thou hast laid him, and I will take him away.

Jesus saith unto her, Mary. She turned herself, and saith unto him, Rabboni; which is to say, Master. Jesus saith unto her, Touch me not; for I am not yet ascended to my Father: but go to my brethren, and say unto them, I ascend unto my Father, and your Father; and to my God, and your God.

John 20:1, 11-17

And they departed quickly from the sepulchre with fear and great joy; and did run to bring his disciples word. And as they went to tell his disciples, behold, Jesus met them, saying, All hail. And they came and held him by the feet, and worshipped him.

Matthew 28:8, 9

And when he had spoken these things, while they beheld, he was taken up; and a cloud received him out of their sight.

Acts 1:9

The true Light, which lighteth every man that cometh into the world, . . .was in the world, . . .and the world knew him not. . . . The Word was made flesh, and dwelt among us, . . . full of grace and truth.

John 1:9, 10, 14

God so loved the world, that he gave his only begotten Son, that whosoever believeth in him should not perish, but have everlasting life. For God sent not his Son into the world to condemn the world; but that the world through him might be saved.

He that believeth on him is not condemned: but he that believeth not is condemned already, because he hath not believed in the name of the only begotten Son of God. And this is the condemnation, that light is come into the world, and men loved darkness rather than light, because their deeds were evil. For every one that doeth evil hateth the light, neither cometh to the light, lest his deeds should be reproved. But he that doeth truth cometh to the light, that his deeds may be made manifest, that they are wrought in God.

John 3:16-21

If we be dead with Christ, we believe that we shall also live with him: knowing that Christ being raised from the dead dieth no more; death hath no more dominion over him. For in that he died, he died unto sin once: but in that he liveth, he liveth unto God.

Romans 6:8-10

I am persuaded, that neither death, nor life, nor angels, nor principalities, nor powers, nor things present, nor things to come, nor height, nor depth, nor any other creature, shall be able to separate us from the love of God, which is in Christ Jesus our Lord.

Romans 8:38, 39

Ye know the grace of our Lord Jesus Christ, that, though he was rich, yet for your sakes he became poor, that ye through his poverty might be rich.

2 Corinthians 8:9

Ye are all the children of God by faith in Christ Jesus. For as many of you as have been baptized into Christ have put on Christ. There is neither Jew nor Greek, there is neither bond nor free, there is neither male nor female: for ye are all one in Christ Jesus.

Galatians 3:26-28

This is a faithful saying, and worthy of all acceptation, that Christ Jesus came into the world to save sinners; of whom I am chief.

1 Timothy 1:15

Let us lay aside every weight, and the sin which doth so easily beset us, and let us run with patience the race that is set before us, looking unto Jesus the author and finisher of our faith; who for the joy that was set before him endured the cross, despising the shame, and is set down at the right hand of the throne of God.

Hebrews 12:1, 2

He is despised and rejected of men; a man of sorrows, and acquainted with grief: and we hid as it were our faces from him. . . . he was wounded for our transgressions, he was bruised for our iniquities: the chastisement of our peace was upon him; and with his stripes we are healed. . . . the Lord hath laid on him the iniquity of us all.

He was oppressed, and he was afflicted, yet he opened not his mouth: he is brought as a lamb to the slaughter, and as a sheep before her shearers is dumb, so he openeth not his mouth. He was taken from prison and from judgment: and who shall declare his generation? for he was cut off out of the land of the living: for the transgression of my people was he stricken. And he made his grave with the wicked, and with the rich in his death; because he had done no violence, neither was any deceit in his mouth.

Isaiah 53:3, 5, 6-9

I can do all things through Christ which strengtheneth me.

Philippians 4:13

PART II

WHAT THEY SAY ABOUT JESUS

ACCEPTANCE

Acceptance

Do you love the Son? Is he the captain of ambition and desire? Are you receiving daily into your spirit those marvelous resources and powers which are available from Christ? Are you living an everlasting life? Are you happy? Are you calm? When you can say Yes to these questions you have come to the point where your partnership with Christ begins.

Alistair MacLean

There are stars aplenty today, but have you seen His star and what are you doing about it?

Vance Havner

Jesus Christ will never strong-arm his way into your life.

Grady B. Wilson

You want to compete with his affection before you have understood it; that is your mistake. . . . Come, then! Show a little more deference to your Lord and allow him to go first. Let him love you a great deal before you have succeeded in loving him even a little as you would wish to love him. That is all that our Lord asks of you.

Henri de Tourville

To know Jesus personally is authentic maturity.

Richard C. Halverson

There are people today who, though they disdain the church, Christianity and religion, have limitless admiration for Jesus Christ, and are ready to listen to what he said and to what is said about him by persons they have learned to respect.

John A. Mackay

You will get to heaven by accepting Christ as Savior, but by accepting Christ as Lord and Savior you will bring heaven down to yourself.

Jordan C. Khan

O Lord, I ain't no stranger now,
O Lord, I ain't no stranger now.
I've been introduced to the Father and the Son,
O Lord, I ain't no stranger now!

Black Spiritual

Learn to commit your soul and the building of it to One who can keep it and build it as you never can.

Peter T. Forsyth

I have a room.
'Tis poor, but 'tis my best, if
  Thou wilt come
Within so small a cell, where I would fain
Mine and the world's Redeemer entertain.
I mean my heart.

Matthew Hale

I came to Christ as a country boy. I did not understand all about the plan of salvation. One does not have to understand it; one has only to stand on it. I do not understand all about electricity, but I do not intend to sit around in the dark until I do! One thing I did understand even as a lad: I understood that I was under new management. I belonged to Christ and he was Lord.

Vance Havner

After six years given to the imperial investigation of Christianity as to its truth or falsity, I have come to the deliberate conclusion that Jesus Christ is the Messiah of the Jews, the Savior of the world, and my personal Savior.

Lee Wallace

I have inevitably and increasingly been driven to the conclusion, almost against my own will, that for a West European whose life and background and tradition are in terms of Western European Christian civilization, the only answer lies in the person and life and teaching of Christ.

Malcolm Muggeridge

The basis of Christ's authority is not a prior belief in his divinity or miracles, but the impression which his Personality makes on us.

R.H. Strachan

Jesus astonishes and overpowers sensual people. They cannot unite Him to history or reconcile Him with themselves.

Ralph Waldo Emerson

Whether it be something tremendously important in our eyes or the greatest triviality, nothing, nothing may be so put between ourselves and Christ that it becomes a condition. For in such a case we cannot surrender ourselves to him. The surrender must be unconditional; then,—and this is a different thing from making prior conditions—we can pray for ourselves that our burden may not be too heavy.

Søren Kierkegaard

Rest in the Lord, and wait patiently for him. In Hebrew, Be silent to God, and let Him mold thee. Keep still, and He will mold thee to the right shape.

Martin Luther

Since the lines have been cleared between the Lord and me, the telephone has never stopped ringing.

Bernard L. Clark

We get no deeper into Christ than we allow him to get into us.

John Henry Jowett

You cannot receive Christ in bits and pieces.

David Martyn Lloyd-Jones

A man can accept what Christ has done without knowing how it works; indeed, he certainly won't know how it works until he's accepted it.

C.S. Lewis

I have prayed in her fields of poppies,
  I have laughed with the men who died—
But in all my ways and through all my days
  Like a friend He walked beside.
I have seen a sight under Heaven
  That only God understands,
In the battle's glare I have seen Christ there
  With the Sword of God in His Hand.

Gordon Johnstone

The Almighty does nothing without reason, though the frail mind of man cannot explain the reason.

St. Augustine of Hippo

How many of us go through life as peasants when we could be walking as royalty in Christ?

Robert Wheatley

B

BROTHERHOOD

Brotherhood

Consider Jesus of Nazareth, the most generous-hearted person who ever lived. He never refused a request for help. Great multitudes followed him, and he healed them all. He went out of his way to cross racial and religious barriers. He compassed the whole world in his love.

Anonymous

I will tell you what to hate. Hate hypocrisy, hate cant, hate intolerance, oppression, injustice; hate Pharisaism; hate them as Christ hated them, with a deep, living, god-like hatred.

Frederick W. Robertson

The modern world began with Christ's discovery of the individual.

John MacMurray

Man becomes a holy thing, a neighbor, only if we realize that he is the property of God and that Jesus Christ died for him.

Helmut Thielicke

The identifying mark of God is organic unity, found functioning preeminently in Jesus, which operates in the world to make us brothers; that is, functional members of one another.

Henry Nelson Wieman

Jesus Christ belonged to the true race of prophets. He saw with open eye the mystery of the soul. Drawn by its severe harmony, ravished with its beauty, he lived in it, and had his being there. Alone in all history he estimated the greatness of man.

Ralph Waldo Emerson

Jesus said love one another. He didn't say love the whole world.

Mother Teresa

Christ did not love humanity. He never said that he loved humanity. He loved men.

Gilbert K. Chesterton

Christ utterly believed and proved with His life that love is more potent than any possible array of mere physical force.

Francis B. Sayre

Bear ye one another's burdens, and so fulfill the law of Christ.

Galatians 6:2

Unless we learn the meaning of mercy by exercising it towards others, we will never have any real knowledge of what it means to love Christ.

Thomas Merton

Beloved, let us love one another: for love is of God; and every one that loveth is born of God, and knoweth God. He that loveth not, knoweth not God; for God is love.

1 John 4:7, 8

Jesus Christ, the Man for Others,
we, your people, make our prayer:
Give us grace to love as brothers
all whose burdens we can share.

Stewart Cross

Anything that has any remote resemblance to discrimination is not only anti-American, but anti-Christian as well. Jesus Christ, the Son of God, declared that second only to the supreme law binding us to love our God is the law binding us to love our neighbor.

Francis J. Haas

Christ came to heal, not to hurt. Prejudice wounds our fellow men. Christians especially should take particular care as we teach His Gospel to avoid sowing seeds of hatred towards those of His own background—or hatred toward any minority group. He died for all.

James A. Pike

When I met Christ at the crossroads of life, he showed me which way to go by walking it with me.

Anonymous

Loving as He loves,
helping as He helps,
giving as He gives,
serving as He serves,
rescuing as he rescues,
being with Him for all the 24 hours,
touching Him in His distressing disguise.

Mother Teresa

I am to become a Christ to my neighbor and be for him what Christ is for me.

Martin Luther

DENIAL

Denial

The fire of Hell is insupportable—who does not know it? —and its torments are awful. But if you were to heap a thousand hell-fires one on top of the other, it would be as nothing compared to the punishment of being excluded from the beatific glory of Heaven, hated by Christ and compelled to hear him say, "I know you not."

St. John Chrysostom

If Christ is born a thousand times in Bethlehem and not in thee, then art thou lost for ever.

Angelus Silesius

It is a faithful saying: For if we be dead with him, we shall also live with him: if we suffer, we shall also reign with him: if we deny him, he also will deny us: if we believe not, yet he abideth faithful: he cannot deny himself.

2 Timothy 2:11-13

Whatever Jesus meant by hell, essentially it is the separation of the soul from God as the culmination of man's spiritual death.

Billy Graham

Two veils keep us from seeing the living truth of Jesus. One veil is our ignorance. . . . The other veil is that we think we know, but in truth we are just accustomed to hearing the same words, episodes, statements over and over again.

Romano Guardini

The Christ had to suffer and die, because whenever the Divine appears in all Its depth, It cannot be endured by men. . . . In the picture of the Crucified, we look at the rejection of the Divine by humanity.

Paul Tillich

If I am not finding Jesus a real Savior, who brings me fully out of darkness and defeat into light and liberty, it is because at one point or another I am not willing to be broken, and see myself as a sinner.

Roy Hession

The witness for the historical authentication and for the proofs of the Divinity of Jesus, from the earliest days, are far more comprehensive than the testimonies for the existence of many famous historical characters we accept without question.

Herbert E. Cory

So you think that God does not exist anywhere? You must have a great deal of knowledge about the universe. Apparently you have examined every nook and corner of it. Logically it is impossible to say, "There is no God." All you can say is "There is no God in my experience." I have found God in Christ. That is my experience. You can have it too. But not your way. You must try God's way.

Akbar Abdul-Haqq

We have greater and sounder ground for believing in the continued life of Christ than the disciples had. . . . We have the overwhelming evidence of nineteen centuries of Christian victories over the world, the flesh and the devil in man.

Rufus M. Jones

The whole of history is incomprehensible without him.

Ernest Renan

Everything in the Kingdom, every spiritual thing, refers to Christ and centers in him.

Isaac Pennington

If I did not see that the Lord kept watch over the ship, I should long since have abandoned the helm. But I see Him! through the storm, strengthening the tackling, handling the yards, spreading the sails—aye more, commanding the very winds! Should I not be a coward if I abandoned my post? Let Him govern, let Him carry us forward, let Him hasten or delay, we will fear nothing.

Martin Luther

Jesus lived so intimately with God that he never thought of proving God's existence, as religious people are so feverishly doing in our day.

W.A. Smart

We do great injustice to Iscariot, in thinking him wicked above all common wickedness. He was only a common money-lover, and like all money-lovers, did not understand Christ.

John Ruskin

The latter period of Judas' life is a frightening illustration of the power of the human will to resist grace. Judas looked upon Christ day after day; he talked with him and supped with him; he slept alongside him under the stars at night. . . . And yet, after more than two years of this, he refuses to open the doors of his soul to the rays of Christ's divine grace.

Ralph Gorman

Betrayer of the Master,
He sways against the sky
A black and broken body,
Iscariot—or I?

Caroline Giltinan

If Jesus Christ were to come today, people would not even crucify him. They would ask him to dinner, and hear what he had to say, and make fun of it.

Thomas Carlyle

The Crucified becomes one with the unrecognized and misused and cruelly treated in every age. The nail-pierced Figure on Calvary haunts our race as a symbol of what is forever taking place generation after generation, and of what each of us has his part in.

William Sloane Coffin

The work of the Lord Jesus . . . is represented by "the blood" shed for our justification through "the remission of sins." The blood deals with what we have done, whereas the cross deals with what we are. The blood disposes of our sins, while the cross strikes at the root of our capacity for sin.

Watchman Nee

God bought men here with His heart's blood expence;
And man sold God here for base thirty pence.

Robert Herrick

The religious charge against him was that he was a blasphemer; the political charge, that he was a traitor. He was executed by "good" people, representing the best interests of a great religious tradition and an enlightened political power. But in the last analysis, no religious, political, ethnic, or other group was primarily responsible for Jesus' death. Offended pride; disappointed hopes; evil exposed by love; the need to destroy that which threatens established securities of private and public life—all of these were at work in the execution of Jesus.

James A. Martin

It is a terrible mistake to understand Jesus as having been crucified by some especially bad people in the first century. Jesus was crucified by the highest reach of human religiousity, morality, and political justice.

Albert T. Mollegen

The Galilean has been too great for our small hearts.

H. G. Wells

Jesus Christ, God and man, lies on His face in the Garden of Gethsemane and sees before Him the cross which His friends prepare for Him. They will do it also tomorrow, the days after tomorrow, all the days until the end of the world.

Sugrud Ybdset

F

FAITH

FATHER, SON, HOLY SPIRIT

FORGIVENESS

FRESH STARTS

Faith

To believe on Christ, I say: not merely to believe in him, or to believe something about him, but to believe on him; and this means to entrust your soul to him and to trust in him for wisdom and strength and salvation.

Washington Gladen

Faith is more than intellectual acceptance of the revelation in Jesus Christ; it is whole-hearted trust in God and His promises, and committal of ourselves to Jesus Christ as Saviour and Lord.

Walter M. Horton

There are some sciences that may be learned by the head, but the sciences of Christ crucified can only be learned by the heart.

Charles H. Spurgeon

To see the revelation of God in Christ is a gracious privilege of faith, of the believer and not of the historian.

Emil Brunner

The faith which Jesus required of men was neither credal adherence nor mystic ecstasy so much as the faith that is in some sort native to every pure and gentle heart—the faith in man, the faith in life, the faith in the power of love, the faith in the Unseen Love of God.

John Baillie

When Jesus healed the man blind from birth, he let him grope his way, still blind, to wash in the pool—and then the light broke. We don't need to know what we're groping toward—or why. It is enough that we have Christ's direction. The light will break in God's own time.

Anonymous

Up to this day no one has ever been loved as much as Jesus Christ is loved and in the future likewise no one will ever be loved as much as He is loved.

Pope Pius XI

God and I have this in common—we both love his Son, Jesus Christ.

Lance Zavitz

Jesus is the rosetta stone in the language of love.

Nora Jane Ison

Sometimes in narrower, sometimes in broader channels, the purpose of love moves on till the Spirit finds in the Son of Man, the anointed One, the perfect realization of the destiny of man, the manhood in which he can freely and fully work.

Charles Gore

He simply wanted to be loved, nothing more. Of course, there are those who love him, even among Christians. But they are not numerous.

Albert Camus

Strong Son of God, immortal Love,
  Whom we, that have not seen thy face,
  By faith, and faith alone, embrace,
Believing where we cannot prove.

Alfred Lord Tennyson

If Christ has grappled our hearts to Himself at all, then it were surely wise to trust His certainties and not our own doubts, however persistent.

H. H. Farmer

Every step toward Christ kills a doubt.

Theodore L. Cuyler

Every story of conversion is the story of a blessed defeat.

C. S. Lewis

The greatest and most profound mysteries of God, hidden from those who go about in the world, however wise they may be, have been revealed to the small and humble in the faith of Jesus.

Nicholas of Cusa

Jesus Christ is no crutch; he is the ground to walk on.

Leighton Ford

You are to conceive of the holy Jesus or the Word of God as the hidden treasure of every human soul, born as a seed of the Word in the birth of the soul.

William Law

There met in Jesus Christ all things that can make man lovely and loveable.

Gerard Manley Hopkins

I cast off the mooring lines at a decaying wharf and pointed the bow toward the open sea of life, trusting my new Captain to take me safely to his heavenly haven.

Roy C. Naden

"Into thy hands." This final word of Jesus brings completion of faith for others, completion of faith for us. Faith in Him leads us at last to trust. We yield our all to Him because we believe what He said about God and life as true.

James W. Kennedy

The most remarkable fact in the whole history of religious thought is this: that when the early Christians looked back and pondered on the dreadful thing that had happened, it made them think of the redeeming love of God.

D.M. Baillie

You can trust the man who died for you.

Lettie Cowman

(Jesus Christ) absolutely trusted the Bible, and though there are in it things inexplicable and intricate that have puzzled me much, I am going to trust the Book, not in a blind sense, but reverently, because of him.

H.C.G. Moule

The whole question of the virgin birth of Jesus need not afflict the average man. If Jesus is unique, unlike any other person, it is not illogical to believe that his birth was unique.

William Lyon Phelps

To believe is to commit . . . . In particular belief I commit myself spiritually to Jesus Christ, and determine in that thing to be dominated by the Lord alone. When I stand face to face with Jesus Christ and he says to me, "Believest thou this?" I find that faith is as natural as breathing, and I am staggered that I was so stupid as not to trust him before.

Oswald Chambers

What can I give Him,
Poor as I am?
If I were a shepherd,
I would bring a lamb;
If I were a wise man,
I would do my part;
Yet what I can I give him—
Give my heart.

Christina Rossetti

More and more, I believe the great spiritual dividing line between men will be the line between those who really accept Christ's ideals and those who do not.

Hastings Rashdall

The King of Love my Shepherd is,
Whose goodness faileth never;
I nothing lack if I am His
And He is mine for ever.

Henry Williams Baker

Theoretically a man can believe in the resurrection . . . without believing in the virgin birth, yet such a halfway conviction is not likely to endure. The virgin birth is an integral part of the New Testament witness about Christ, and that witness is strongest when it is taken as it stands.

J. Gresham Machen

Christ came not to be ministered to, but to minister; and our first duty, therefore, is to be ministered to by him. First faith, then works.

Peter T. Forsyth

If every person in the world had adequate food, housing, income; if all men were equal; if every possible social evil and injustice were done away with, men would still need one thing: Christ!

J.W. Hyde

Father, Son, Holy Spirit

The most unique things to my mind about the Jesus of history is . . . a new and most wonderfully rich experience of God that apparently had been growing and deepending through all those silent background years.

J.S. Bonnell

The eternal wisdom of God . . . has shown itself forth in all things, but chiefly in the mind of man, and most of all in Jesus Christ.

Baruch Spinoza

Others had applied the name "Father" to God, but the point is that when Jesus called God Father he knew him as the Father.

Bruce M. Metzger

If the character which is revealed by that Sufferer be the character of God Himself, then the love that is awakened towards Christ will also be the love of the Father whom in a supreme and unique way Christ reveals.

Hastings Rashdall

Having made known unto us the mystery of his will, . . . he might gather together in one all things in Christ, both which are in heaven, and which are on earth.

Ephesians 1:9, 10

[Jesus] was transfigured before them: and his face did shine as the sun, and his raiment was white as the light . . . . A bright cloud overshadowed them: and behold a voice out of the cloud, which said, This is my beloved Son, in whom I am well pleased; hear ye him.

Matthew 17:2, 5

Christ attributes all he does and says to the Father, and this makes God's name no longer terrible to us, but comforting.

Martin Luther

For it pleased the Father that in him should all fullness dwell; and, having made peace through the blood of his cross, by him to reconcile all things unto himself; by him, I say, whether they be things in earth, or things in heaven.

Colossians 1:19, 20

God cared so much about man's renewal that he sent his Son into the world to accomplish this purpose.

W. Curry Mavis

Thou art the King of Glory O Christ.
Thou art the everlasting Son of the Father.

Book of Common Prayer

I believe Jesus Christ to be the Son of God. The miracles which he wrought establish in my mind, his personal authority, and render it proper for me to believe whatever he asserts. I believe, therefore, all his declarations, as well when he declares himself to be the Son of God, as when he declares any other proposition. And I believe there is no other way of salvation than through the merits of his atonement.

Daniel Webster

Our age has fortunately rediscovered the extraordinarily brotherly character of the Son of Man but misses the mystery of the Son of God.

Emmanuel Suhard

The best picture we can ever acquire of God is that afforded by the person of Jesus Christ, the untarnished mirror of the Most High.

John A. O'Brien

Jesus Christ (is) the condescension of divinity and the exaltation of humanity.

Phillips Brooks

[Christ] is the image of the invisible God, the firstborn of every creature.

Colossians 1:15

From our proper Ground, that is to say from the Father and all that which lives in Him, there shines an eternal Ray, which is the Birth of the Son.

John Ruysbroeck

Yes, if the life and death of Socrates were those of a sage, the life and death of Jesus are those of a God.

Jean Jacques Rousseau

None but the God we see in Jesus Christ will meet men's case.

Arthur John Gossip

Was He sent, think you, as any man might suppose, to establish a sovereignty, to inspire fear and terror? Not so. But in gentleness and meekness had He sent Him, as a king might send his son who is a king. He sent Him, as sending God; He sent Him, as a man unto men; He sent Him, as Saviour, as using persuasion, not force.

Epistle to Diognetus, c. 200

No man hath seen God at any time; the only begotten Son, which is in the bosom of the Father, he hath declared him.

John 1:18

They should have known that (Christ) was God. His patience should have proved that to them.

Tertullian

We could never recognize the Father's grace and mercy except our Lord Jesus Christ, who is a mirror of His Father's heart.

Martin Luther

Jesus has sometimes been represented as being merely a teacher of morality, but if he had been that and nothing more there would have been no reason for the Pharisees to have feared him.

Marchette Chute

A man who was merely a man and said the sort of things Jesus said wouldn't be a great moral teacher. He'd either be a lunatic—on a level with a man who says he's a poached egg—or else he'd be the Devil of Hell. You must make your choice. Either this man was, and is, the Son of God, or else a madman or something worse.

C.S. Lewis

The Core of the Christian revelation is that Jesus Christ is the sole legitimate Lord of all human lives.

Hendrick Kraemer

The Son of God is unique. To appear for a moment, to flash forth a sympathetic but piercing radiance, to die very young, that is the life of a God.

Ernest Renan

(Jesus) does not have to rely on the authority of the past or on other teachers. It is in himself. He acts with the manifest authority of God; he is the creative Word of God. In him we are to see what is the purpose of God in making the world and in making us.

William Temple

Jesus Christ is not the best human being, he is a being who cannot be accounted for by the human race at all. He is not man becoming God, but God Incarnate, God coming into human flesh, coming into it from outside. His life is the highest and the holiest entering in at the lowliest door.

Oswald Chambers

What does the Church think of Christ? The Church's answer is categorical and uncompromising, and it is this: That Jesus Bar-Joseph, the carpenter of Nazareth, was in fact and in truth, and in the most exact and literal sense of the words, the God 'by whom all things were made.' His body and brain were those of a common man; His personality was the personality of God, so far as that personality could be expressed in human terms. He was in every respect a genuine living man. He was not merely a man so good as to be 'like God'—He was God.

Dorothy L. Sayers

It seems, then that the form of the earthly, no less than the heavenly Christ is for the most part hidden from us. For all the inestimable value of the Gospels, they yield us little more than a whisper of his voice; we trace in them but the outskirts of his ways.

R.H. Lightfoot

Jesus is still unique because God who breaks through Him is unique, and Jesus is the standard by which all others are measured.

James A. Pike

The mystery of Jesus remains, even so, as deep in its essence for Paul or an Augustine, for an Aquinas or a Newman, as it is for the most resolute and determined unbeliever.

L. de Grandmaison

That Christ should be and should be Christ appears the one reasonable, natural certain thing in all the universe. In Him all broken lines unite; in Him all scattered sounds are gathered into harmony.

Phillips Brooks

Only a Christ could have conceived a Christ.

Joseph Parker

Therefore let all the house of Israel know assuredly, that God hath made that same Jesus, whom ye have crucified, both Lord and Christ.

Acts 2:36

Effectual calling is the work of God's Spirit, whereby, convincing us of our sin and misery, enlightening our minds in the knowledge of Christ, and renewing our wills, he doth persuade and enable us to embrace Jesus Christ freely offered to us in the Gospel.

The Westminster Shorter Catechism

God had an only Son, and he was a missionary and a physician.

David Livingstone

The Son according to his Divinity, is coequal and consubstantial with the Father, true God.

Henry Bullinger

In every real encounter with life and with our fellow men we meet the living Spirit, the Creator of life. God is not to be found by leaving the world. He is not found by staying in the world. But those who in their daily living respond with their whole being to the "Thou" by whom they find themselves addressed are caught up into union with the true life of the world.

John H. Oldham

The Holy Spirit Who is the love whereby the Father loves the Son, is also the love whereby God loves creatures and imparts to them His goodness.

St. Thomas Aquinas

What is it that Jesus knew, and what is it that he had seen in his own experience, that was hidden from the kings and prophets? It is condensed in a very brief formula—The kingdom of heaven is in us.

V.G. Simkhovitch

Christ stimulates us, as other great men stimulate us, but we find a power coming from Him into our lives that enables us to respond. That is the experience that proves Him to be the universal Spirit. It does not happen with others.

William Temple

When you come to Christ, the Holy Spirit takes up residence in your heart. Something new is added to your life supernaturally. You are transformed by the renewing of your mind. A new power, a new dimension, a new ability to love, a new joy, a new peace—the Holy Spirit comes in and lives the Christian life through you.

Billy Graham

Christ exists and Spirit and I myself am spirit too; since through the spirit I can reach Him, and through Him reach God, for He is both man and God and since, after all, I was conceived in God's likeness, and the presence of Christ in our midst is formal proof of this fact.

Charles F. Ramuz

The Lord's goodness surrounds us at every moment. I walk through it almost with difficulty, as through thick grass and flowers.

R.W. Barbour

Forgiveness

The Lord's Supper testifies to us that we have complete forgiveness of all our sins through the one sacrifice of Jesus Christ which he himself has accomplished on the cross once and for all.

The Heidelberg Catechism

I think I may have to go through the agony of hearing all my sins recited in the presence of God. But I believe it will be like this—Jesus will come over and lay his hand across my shoulders and say to God, "Yes, all these things are true, but I'm here to cover up for Peter. He is sorry for all his sins, and by a transaction made between us, I am now solely responsible for them."

Peter Marshall

Though our Savior's Passion is over, his compassion is not.

William Penn

Nothing in this lost world bears the press of the Son of God so surely as forgiveness.

Alice Cary

Christ saved one thief at the last gasp, to show that there may be late repentance.

John Donne

This calm assumption of Jesus that he is not a sinner will take hold of the wrists of any thoughtful mind and twist them till it must come to its knees.

William A. Quayle

Here is pictured for us all the spirit of Compassionate Goodness at the heart of reality.

Harold Blake Walker

The fall of man has led to a condition of incompleteness. Unregenerate man is spiritually incomplete, for he is out of touch with God. He is morally incomplete, for he lacks both the final standard of conduct which is the will of God, and the dynamic which is the indwelling of God's Spirit. He is mentally incomplete, for sin has vitiated even his reasoning power, and he cannot understand spiritual truths. Only through the miracle of regeneration in which, through union with Christ, he partakes of the life of God, does he reach his completeness.

Herbert M. Carson

For in that he himself hath suffered being tempted, he is able to succor them that are tempted.

Hebrews 2:18

Jesus said, "If ye forgive men their trespasses, your heavenly Father will also forgive you." This can only mean that the reason we should urge for our own forgiveness is that we have forgiven others. It might even mean that the measure of forgiveness we should demand is the measure of forgiveness we have granted.

Robert Keable

Is it not a shame that we are always afraid of Christ, whereas there was never in heaven or earth a more loving, familiar, or milder man, in words, works and demeanour, especially towards poor, sorrowful and tormented consciences?

Martin Luther

For none of us liveth to himself, and no man dieth to himself. For whether we live, we live unto the Lord; and whether we die, we die unto the Lord: whether we live therefore, or die, we are the Lord's.

So then every one of us shall give account of himself to God.

Romans 14:7, 8, 12

There is a type of person who doesn't go to church because he has sinned. In Christ's estimation that is the person who has one added reason for being in church.

Sebastian Miklas

I was going to waste until Jesus recycled me.

Richelle Cross

After I received him, Jesus restored my identity, filled my longing, erased my guilt and shame, and washed me from my sins.

Justine Kovar

He was exactly what the man with a delusion never is; he was wise; he was a good judge.

Gilbert K. Chesterton

He knew all men, and needed not that any should testify of man; for he knew what was in man.

John 2:24, 25

I know Thee, Saviour, who Thou art,
Jesus, the feeble sinner's Friend;
Nor wilt Thou with the night depart,
But stay and love me to the end:
Thy mercies never shall remove;
Thy nature and Thy name is Love.

Charles Wesley

Rarely, almost never, do we see the vast divinity within that soul, which, new though it was in the flesh, at one step goes before the world whole thousands of years; judges the race; decides for us questions we dare not agitate as yet, and breathes the very breath of heavenly love.

Theodore Parker

I thank Christ Jesus our Lord, who hath enabled me, for that he counted me faithful, putting me into the ministry; who was before a blasphemer, and a persecutor, and injurious: but I obtained mercy.

1 Timothy 1:12, 13

He taught me all the mercy,
For He sho'd me all the sin.
Now, tho' my lamp was lighted late,
There's One will let me in.

Alfred Lord Tennyson

Fresh Starts

Jesus called for radical change and revolution, for an absolutely new beginning. He still does. He demands repentance, faith and obedience. This Revolutionary is calling you to a revolutionary experience with himself.

Ralph S. Bell

Modern youth alternates between abysmal hang-ups and fanatical commitments. Psychologists call their malady an "identity crisis." Its chief symptom is the cry: "Who am I? To them I say, Have a confrontation with yourself. Then have a confrontation with Jesus Christ. Join the Jesus Generation and find your true identity in him."

Billy Graham

Just as Jesus Christ found it necessary to sweep the moneychangers from the Temple porch, so we ourselves need a lot of housecleaning.

Dale Evans Rogers

The Lord is telling us to be honest about our sins, to put away bitterness, criticism, and dishonesty from among us. Christ must have first place in our lives. We need to give him the key to every secret closet in our hearts, and help him to clean out all the junk we have allowed to accumulate there.

Carol Myers

When I was saved, I accepted death as my only deliverance. Christ died in my place. I was indeed a dead man but for Christ. When I accepted Christ's death for my sin, I could not avoid accepting my own death to sin. I am committed to the cross. My only logical standing is one of death. I have been "born crucified."

L.E. Maxwell

Jesus obliged us to confess our sins for our own sake rather than for his. . . . If you harm a friend, it is not enough to apologize to God—you must apologize to your friend as well.

Alfred Wilson

We believe that the first time we're born, as children, it's human life given to us; and when we accept Jesus as our Savior, it's a new life. That's what "born again" means.

Jimmy Carter

I was a sour note on Adam's reed when the Master Musician reorchestrated my life and gave the angels something to sing about.

Nancy Thomas

And they come to Jesus, and see him that was possessed with the devil, and had the legion, sitting, and clothed, and in his right mind; and they were afraid.

Mark 5:15

When the love of Christ comes into a human life it is the greatest uplifting and ennobling power of which the world has any knowledge. It brings new birth, for it brings Christ himself. For it no sacrifice is too great, no piece of service too humble.

Howard W. Guinness

Nothing accords better with the nature of man than the philosophy of Christ, of which the sole end is to give back to fallen nature its innocence and integrity.

Desiderius Erasmus

Jesus . . . bore within him the germs of a new social and political order. He was too great to be the Saviour of a fractional part of human life.

Walter Rauschenbusch

I am amazed by the sayings of Christ. They seem truer than anything I have ever read. And they certainly turn the world upside down.

Katharine Butler Hathaway

One of the things Jesus did was to step aside from the organized religion of his time because it had become corrupt and bogged down with rules. Rules became more important than feeding the hungry.

Corita Kent

Jesus Christ is the only platform from which a true radical, revolutionary program can be launched. . . . If you want to radicalize the world; if you want to radicalize your church; if you want to see things changed, you must begin with a change in yourself. Come to Christ and let him live his life through you.

Tom Skinner

Caesar hoped to reform men by changing institutions and laws; Christ wished to remake institutions, and lessen laws, by changing men.

Will Durant

Christ must be rediscovered perpetually.

Edith Hamilton

By his first work He gave me to myself; and by the next He gave Himself to me. And when He gave Himself, He gave me back myself that I had lost.

St. Bernard of Clairvaux

Therefore if any man be in Christ, he is a new creature: old things are passed away; behold, all things are become new.

2 Corinthians 5:17

The torn garments of our world can be rewoven only through the expert invisible mending of the greatest Tailor of all time, Jesus Christ.

Bonnie Zandr

Christ came when all things were growing old. He made them new.

St. Augustine of Hippo

I

INSPIRATION

Inspiration

The Son of God came into the world not only by his doctrine to instruct us in the way to happiness, and by his death to make expiation of sin, but by his life to be an example to us of holiness and virtue.

Archbishop Tillotson

Jesus remains the very heart and soul of the Christian movement, still controlling men, still capturing men—against their wills very often—changing men's lives and using them for ends they never dreamed of.

T.R. Glover

We must make it plain that the Christian demand for justice does not come from Karl Marx. It comes from Jesus Christ and the Hebrew prophets.

G. Bromley Oxnam

Jesus Christ didn't come into my heart to sit down; he started moving around.

Andy Hamilton

Before Christ, a man loves things and uses people. After Christ, he loves people and uses things.

Horace Wood

Christ . . . does not really teach one anything, but by being brought into his presence one becomes something. And everybody is predestined to his presence. Once at least in his life each man walks with Christ to Emmaus.

Oscar Wilde

If Christ lives in us, controlling our personalities, we will leave glorious marks on the lives we touch. Not because of our lovely characters, but because of his.

Eugenia Price

His love, at once, and dread, instruct our thought;
As man He suffered, and as God he taught.

Edmund Waller

Jesus alone is able to offer himself as the sufficient illustration of his own doctrine.

Herbert Hensley Henson

Jesus clothes the Beatitudes with his own life.

Carl F.H. Henry

Christ did not find heroism in everyone; whoever showed but a trace of good will, to him He tendered His hand and inspired him with courage.

Pope Pius XII

It is wonderful never to have read or known anything about the teachings of Christ until you have found that in spite of your proud intellect and your worldly experience and your artistic insight you are defeated and helpless. Then they do seem like the flowers of spring—for freshness and miraculous beauty and so much more besides.

Katharine Butler Hathaway

The healing of His seamless dress
Is by our beds of pain;
We touch Him in life's throng and press,
And we are whole again.

John Greenleaf Whittier

Every thought, word and deed, for Christ carries you away from discouragement.

Theodore L. Cuyler

To satisfy the burning thirst of tormented souls nothing will do but to take them to the well of living waters, to true fellowship with Christ.

Paul Tournier

Christ is rich, who will maintain you: He opens at once the eye of conscience to perceive and know the pure and holy God the Father that dwelt in him and made him so full of truth and grace.

James Martineau

The whole teaching of Jesus is grounded in what may be termed an ethical mysticism. He is possessed with the thought of love and goodness as so inherent in divine nature that by attaining to them we apprehend God.

Ernest F. Scott

How else but through a broken heart may Lord Christ enter his?

Oscar Wilde

He kindled a flame which was to burn more brightly after his death than ever before it in his lifetime.

Claude G. Montefiore

Christ, like all fascinating personalities had the power of not merely saying beautiful things himself, but of making other people say beautiful things to him.

Oscar Wilde

His genius, though he wrote nothing, was that of a great literary artist; if it were not for the sound of the thing, one might say that he was the master rhetorician of religion.

Paul Elmer More

A great teacher of morality and an artist in parable.

Joseph Klausner

History shows that Christ on the cross has been more potent than anything else in arousing a compassion for suffering and indignation of injustice.

F.J. Foakes-Jackson

Most men find in Jesus a reflection of their own ideals.

Granville Hicks

Everything that is tender, that is sensitive, that is movingly beautiful in modernity, comes from Christ.

Edmond and Jules de Goncourt

The gentleness of Christ is the comeliest ornament that a Christian can wear.

William Arnot

I find the name of Jesus Christ written on the top of every page of modern history.

George Bancroft

All that is best in the civilization of today is the fruit of Christ's appearance among men.

Daniel Webster

In him was life; and the life was the light of men.

John 1:4

This is the way Jesus saves us: by revealing the nature of God and by creating within us the desire for fellowship with Him; by exhibiting life as it ought to be and may be and thus inspiring us to nobler conduct.

Kirby Page

The influence of His life, His words, and His death, have, from the first, been like heaven cast into the mass of humanity.

Cunningham Geikie

He is all the world's hero, the desire of nations. But besides he is the hero of single souls.

Gerard Manley Hopkins

He became what we are that he might make us what he is.

Athanasius

I've never done anything perfect, I'd like to be perfect, like Christ. Of course it's impossible, but you keep trying.

John Lennon

Him evermore I behold
Walking in Galilee,
Through the cornfield's waving gold,
In hamlet or grassy world,
By the shores of the beautiful Sea.
He toucheth the sightless eyes;
Before Him the demons flee;
To the dead He sayeth: Arise!
To the living: Follow me!
And that voice still soundeth on
From the centuries that are gone,
To the centuries that shall be!

Henry Wadsworth Longfellow

K

KINGDOM OF HEAVEN

Kingdom of Heaven

A time of great light and knowledge . . . it (the Kingdom of Heaven on Earth) shall be a time of great holiness . . . it will be a time of excellent order in the church of Christ . . . ease, quietness, pleasantness, and cheerfullness of mind, also wealth and a great increase of children . . . temporal prosperity will be promoted by a remarkable blessing from heaven.

Jonathan Edwards

Our world is filled with fear, hate, lust, greed, war and utter despair. Surely the Second Coming of Jesus Christ is the only hope of replacing these depressing features with trust, love, universal peace and prosperity. For it the world wittingly or inadvertently waits.

Billy Graham

This doctrine of the Kingdom of Heaven, which was the main teaching of Jesus . . . is certainly the most revolutionary doctrine that ever stirred and changed human thought . . . no less than a bold and uncompromising demand for a complete change and cleansing of the life of our struggling race.

H.G. Wells

The Lord hath opened to me by His invisible power how that every man was enlightened by the divine Light of Christ; and I saw it shine through all; and they that believed in it came out of condemnation and came to the Light of Life, and became the children of it.

George Fox

With a width and wonder of imagination that fills one almost with awe, he took the entire world of the inarticulate, the voiceless world of pain, as his kingdom, and made of himself its external mouthpiece.

Oscar Wilde

In politics He was a leveller or communist; in morals He was a monk; He believed that only the poor and despised would inherit the kingdom of God.

W. Winwood Reade

By the Kingdom of God Jesus meant an ideal (though progressively approximated) social order in which the relation of men to God is that of sons, and therefore to each other, that of brothers.

Shailer Matthews

Our business on earth is to be colonizers of heaven, to redeem the world and set up in it an order of life which will incarnate the spirit and principles of Jesus.

Halford E. Luccock

Jesus, the Saviour, reigns,
The God of truth and love;
When He had purged our stains,
He took His seat above:
Lift up your heart, lift up your voice:
Rejoice; again I say, 'Rejoice.'

Charles Wesley

A man may go to heaven without health, without riches, without honors, without learning, without friends; but he can never go there without Christ.

John Dyer

The dead in Christ shall rise first: then we which are alive and remain shall be caught up together with them in the clouds, to meet the Lord in the air: and so shall we ever be with the Lord.

1 Thessalonians 4:16, 17

Christ designed that the day of his coming should be hid from us, that being in suspense, we might be as it were upon the watch.

Martin Luther

The attitude toward death is changing in our modern thinking. No longer is it something to be feared, but rather a giving of ourselves united with Christ.

Clifford Howell

We were chaff, now we are wheat; we were dross, now we are gold; we were ravens, now we are doves; we were goats, now we are sheep; we were thorns, now we are grapes; we were thistles, now we are lilies; we were strangers, now we are citizens; we were harlots, now we are virgins; hell was our inheritance, now heaven is our possession; we were children of wrath, now we are sons of mercy; we were bondslaves to Satan, now we are heirs of God and co-heirs with Jesus Christ.

James Bisse

I'm going to heaven and I believe I'm going by the blood of Christ. That's not popular preaching, but I'll tell you it's all the way through the Bible and I may be the last fellow on earth who preaches it, but I'm going to preach it because it's the only way we're going to get there.

Billy Graham

I do understand enough about myself to know that when I get to heaven I'll be overjoyed just to stand in line, knowing at last I'm in His presence. His love does this to us. Love that is always giving. Oh, I just love Him. I love Him. How I long for you children to love Him too.

Ethel Waters

What definition did Jesus give of "success"? He said that true success is to complete one's life. It is to attain to eternal life; all else is failure.

Toyohiko Kagawa

Man is soon changed and lightly falleth away, but Christ abideth for ever and standeth strongly with his lover unto the end.

Thomas à Kempis

This same Jesus, which is taken up from you into heaven, shall so come in like manner as ye have seen him go into heaven.

Acts 1:11

The hour is coming, in the which all that are in the graves shall hear his voice, and shall come forth.

John 5:28, 29

Only when the kingdom of God on earth is merged into the kingdom of God in heaven will Jesus be able to say of his role of Savior, "It is consummated."

Ralph Gorman

P

POWER AND GLORY PRAYING

Power and Glory

If Jesus of Nazareth is not God, how is it that, without any help, this sacrilegious Seducer has prevailed against the laws of his country, against princes, against wise men, against the whole universe in opposition to him, against the powers of heaven and hell, in fine, against God Himself, even so far as to make himself equal to God, to receive honors due only to Divinity, and to fulfill with an infinite success, in spite of difficulties, and the contradictions generated by long centuries, all the prophecies.

Jerome Savonarola

(Jesus Christ), being the holiest among the mighty, the mightiest among the holy, lifted with his pierced hand empires off their hinges, and the stream of centuries out of its channel, and still governs the ages.

Jean Paul Richter

Commander-in-chief of the Celestial Army, King of Zion, Eternal Emperor, Pontifex Maximus of the Christian Church, Archbishop of All Souls, Elector of Truth, Archduke of Glory, Duke of Life, Prince of Peace, Defender of the gates of Hell, Conqueror of Death, Hereditary Lord of the Sacred Council of the Heavenly Father.

Anonymous

The Kingly Rule of Christ extends not merely over the Church as the congregation of the faithful but, . . .over the whole of the universe in all its heights and depths; and it also confronts and overrules with sovereign dignity the principalities and powers and evil spirits of this World.

Karl Barth

No man can do these miracles that thou doest, except God be with him.

John 3:2

After reading the doctrines of Plato, Socrates or Aristotle, we feel the specific difference between their words and Christ's is the difference between an inquiry and a revelation.

Joseph Parker

All the wisdom in the world and all human cleverness compared with the infinite wisdom of God is sheer and extreme ignorance.

St. John of the Cross

Thou hast conquered, O pale Galilean!
The world has grown grey from thy breath.

Algernon C. Swinburne

Our civilization cannot survive materially unless it be redeemed spiritually with the Spirit of Christ.

Woodrow Wilson

All doctrines of Christianity, however widely they may otherwise diverge philosophically or mythically, are yet at one in seeking in him (Jesus) and his appearance the centre of the world's history.

Wilhelm Windelband

Alexander, Caesar, Charlemagne, and I have founded empires. But on what did we rest the creations of our genius? Upon force. Jesus Christ founded his empire upon love; and at this hour millions of men would die for him.

Napoleon Bonaparte

No, we can never think that Jesus died in despair—or "of a broken heart" as some have said. He was dying in victory, not defeat. He foresaw, if anyone ever did, that future which is more real than the present.

Frederick C. Grant

Remember the triumphant Christian does not fight for victory, he celebrates a victory already won. The victorious life is Christ's business, not yours.

Reginald Wallis

We are more than conquerors through him that loved us.

Romans 8:37

A mighty fortress is our God,
A bulwark never failing;
Our helper He amid the flood
Of Mortal ills prevailing.
For still our ancient foe
Doth seek to work us woe—
His craft and power are great,
And armed with cruel hate.
On earth is not His equal.

Did we in our own strength confide,
Our striving would be losing,
Were not the right man on our side,
The man of God's own choosing.
Dost ask who that may be?
Christ Jesus, it is He—
Lord Sabaoth His name,
From age to age the same,
And He must win the battle.

Martin Luther

Jesus Christ will be Lord of all or he will not be Lord at all.

St. Augustine of Hippo

The Christian faith is not one of cold intellect; rather it is full of love, grace and humanity. It has the strength and compassion with which Christ was able to change the course of human life from evil to good, from selfishness to service, from despair to faith in the highest.

William T. Manning

Whatever may be the surprises of the future, Jesus will never be surpassed. His worship will grow young without ceasing; his legend will call forth tears without end; his sufferings will melt the noblest hearts; all ages will proclaim that among the sons of men there is none born greater than Jesus.

Ernest Renan

Jesus marks the point in history at which it becomes possible for man to adopt consciously as his own purpose the purpose which is already inherent in his own nature.

John MacMurray

He is an abyss filled with light. One must close one's eyes if one is not to fall into it.

Frank Kafka

It is light that enables us to see the differences between things; and it is Christ that gives us light.

Julius and Augustus Hare

Christ is all, and in all.

Colossians 3:11

The head that once was crowned with thorns
Is crowned with glory now.

Thomas Kelley

His parentage was obscure; His condition poor; His education null; His natural endowments meek, benevolent, patient, firm, disinterested, and of the sublimest eloquence.

Thomas Jefferson

Christ is greater than our faith in him.

James Hastings

His life, his spirit, his personality, is incomparably greater than anything he said, or did, or taught.

Rufus M. Jones

Jesus was himself the one convincing and permanent miracle.

Ian McClaren

Poor was his station, laborious his life, bitter his ending; through poverty, through labor, through crucifixion his majesty of nature more shines.

Gerard Manley Hopkins

There are also many other things which Jesus did, the which, if they should be written every one, I suppose that even the world itself could not contain the books that should be written.

John 21:25

He realized in the entire sphere of human relations that imaginative sympathy which in the sphere of Art is the sole secret of creation. He understood the leprosy of the leper, the darkness of the blind, the fierce misery of those who live for pleasure, the strange poverty of the rich.

Oscar Wilde

Cana of Galilee. . . . Ah, that sweet miracle! It was not men's grief, but their joy Christ visited, He worked his first miracle to help men's gladness.

Fedor Dostoevsky

Jesus Christ came into my prison cell last night, and every stone flashed like a ruby.

Samuel Rutherford

I see His blood upon the rose
And in the stars the glory of His eyes,
His body gleams amid eternal snows,
His tears fall from the skies.

Joseph M. Plunkett

When Jesus Christ utters a word, He opens His mouth so wide that it embraces all Heaven and earth even though that word be but in a whisper.

Martin Luther

Christ is the great central fact in the world's history. To him everything looks forward or backward. All the lines of history converge upon him. All the great purposes of God culminate in him. The greatest and the most momentous fact which the history of the world records is the fact of his birth.

Charles H. Spurgeon

And the Word was made flesh, and dwelt among us, (and we beheld his glory, the glory as of the only begotten of the Father), full of grace and truth.

John 1:14

All things were created by him, and for him.

Colossians 1:16

Mine eyes have seen the glory of the coming of the Lord;
He is trampling out the vintage where the grapes of wrath are stored;
He hath loosed the fateful lightning of His terrible swift sword;
His truth is marching on.

Julia Ward Howe

Praying

O Saviour Christ, Thou too art Man;
Thou hast been troubled, tempted, tried;
Thy kind but searching glance can scan
The very wounds that shame would hide;
Thy touch has still its ancient power;
No word from Thee can fruitless fall;
Hear in this solemn evening hour,
And in Thy mercy heal us all.

Henry Twells

Make me a captive, Lord,
And then I shall be free;
Force me to render up my sword,
And I shall conqueror be.
I sink in life's alarms
When by myself I stand;
Imprison me within Thy arms,
And strong shall be my Hand.

George Matheson

Speak to Him, thou, for He hears, and spirit with Spirit can meet—
Closer is He than breathing, and nearer than hands and feet.

Alfred Lord Tennyson

Dear Master, in whose life I see
All that I would but fail to be,
Let Thy clear light for ever shine,
To shame and guide this life of mine.
Though what I dream and what I do
In my weak days are always two,
Help me, oppressed by things undone,
O Thou, whose deeds and dreams are one!

John Hunter

O Lord Jesus Christ, Who art the Way, the Truth, and the Life, we pray Thee suffer us not to stray from Thee who art the Way, nor to distrust Thee, who art the Truth, nor to rest in any other thing than Thee, who art the Life. Teach us by Thy Holy Spirit what to believe, what to do, and wherein to take our rest.

Desiderius Erasmus

Govern all Thy wisdom, O Lord, so that my soul may always be serving Thee as Thou dost will, and not as I may choose. Do not punish me, I beseech Thee, by granting that which I wish or ask, if it offend Thy love, which would always live in me. Let me die to myself, that I may serve Thee: let me live to Thee, who in Thyself art the true Life.

St. Teresa of Avila

One only asks God to do through another what he is willing for the Lord to do through him. That is the law of intercession on every level of life. Only so far as we have been tested and proved willing to do a thing ourselves can we intercede for others. Christ is an Intercessor, because he took the place of each one prayed for. We are never called to intercede for sin—that has been done once and for all; but we are often called to intercede for sinners and their needs, and the Holy Spirit can never "bind the strong man" through us on a higher level than that in which he has first had victory in us.

Rees Howells

We know that God's nature is unchangeable; we are sure that his will is equally so? Is the wish, the submitted wish of a human heart, able to alter the counsel of the Almighty? Can the humble request of believing lips restrain, accelerate, change the settled order of events? Can prayer make things that are not to be as though they were? Yes, a thousand times yes! Intercession is the mother tongue of the whole family of Christ.

Dora Greenwell

The prayer that we find hardest to comprehend, namely, the intercessory, Jesus took most easily and naturally for granted.

Francis J. McConnell

[Jesus] withdrew himself into the wilderness, and prayed.

Luke 5:16

To intercede means literally "to pass between". . . . How the intercession of Christ is conducted, it does not become us either anxiously to inquire, or dogmatically to affirm. . . . Among the innumerable multitude of the chosen of God, not one shall be committed. Nor is it for all in the mass that the Savior makes intercession. He prays for each by himself. With infinite compassion and skill is every special case of each individual presented by this divine Advocate to his Father.

William Symington

Well spake that soldier who being asked what he would do if he became too weak to cling to Christ answered, "Then I will pray Him to cling to me."

Christina Rossetti

Little Jesus, was Thou shy
Once, and just so small as I?
And what did it feel like to be
Out of Heaven, and just like me?

Francis Thompson

So too with prayer in the name of Jesus, Jesus assumes the responsibility and all the consequences. He steps forward for us, steps into the place of the person praying.

Søren Kierkegaard

If you will pray in union to Jesus, having childlike confidence toward God, having the spirit of adoption, crying Abba within you, seeking the glory of God more than all personal benefits, I believe that in all such cases you will get the very thing you ask, at the very time you ask it. Before you call, God will answer; and while you are speaking, he will hear. God will either give you what you ask, or something far better.

Robert Murray McCheyne

It is sheer nonsense for us to imagine that we can learn the high art of getting guidance through communion with the Lord without being willing to set aside time for it. It is no accident that the Bible speaks of prayer as a form of waiting on God.

Paul S. Rees

Approach, my soul, the mercy-seat,
Where Jesus answers prayer;
There humbly fall before His feet,
For none can perish there.

John Newton

Talk to him in prayer of all your wants, your troubles, even of the weariness you feel in serving him. You cannot speak too freely, too trustfully to him.

François Fénelon

Jesus our Lord, and Shepherd of men, caring for
human needs;
Feeding the hungry, healing the sick, showing
your love in deeds;
Help us in your great work to share;
People in want still need your care.
Lord, we are called to follow you;
This we ask strength to do.

Patrick Appleford

Come my soul, thy suit prepare;
Jesus loves to answer prayer;
He himself has bid thee pray,
Therefore will not say thee nay.

John Newton

When we come to Christ's table to commune, we come with a prayer that we may be filled with the fullness of his life, may grow into his likeness, and may evermore dwell in him and he in us.

Howard W. Ellis

This is the confidence that we have in him, that, if we ask any thing according to his will, he heareth us.

1 John 5:14

Christ be with me, Christ before me, Christ behind me,
Christ in me, Christ beneath me, Christ above me,
Christ on my right, Christ on my left,
Christ when I lie down, Christ when I sit down, Christ
when I arise.
Christ in the heart of every man who thinks of me,
Christ in the mouth of every one who speaks of me,
Christ in every eye that sees me,
Christ in every ear that hears me.

St. Patrick

Whatsoever we ask, we receive of him, because we keep his commandments, and do those things that are pleasing in his sight.

1 John 3:22

Nobody knows the trouble I've seen, Nobody knows but Jesus.

Anonymous

O Christ, whose touch unveiled the blind,
Whose presence warmed the lonely soul;
Your love made broken sinners whole,
Your faith cast devils from the mind.
Grant us your faith, your love, your care
To bring to sufferers everywhere.

H.C.A. Gaunt

Be Thou my Vision,
O Lord of my heart;
Naught be all else to me,
Save that Thou art,—
Thou my best thought,
By day and by night,
Waking or sleeping,
Thy presence my light.

Ancient Irish hymn

Jesus, Thou Joy of loving hearts
Thou Fount of life, Thou Light of men,
From the best bliss that earth imparts
We turn unfilled to Thee again.

St. Bernard of Clairvaux

O most merciful Redeemer, Friend, and Brother,
May we know Thee more clearly,
Love Thee more dearly,
Follow Thee more nearly;
For ever and ever.

St. Richard of Chichester

R

RESURRECTION
REWARD

Resurrection

The Son of God was crucified; I am not ashamed because men must needs be ashamed of it, the Son of God died; it is by all means to be believed, because it is absurd. And He was buried and rose again; it is certain, because it is impossible.

Tertullian

Christ's resurrection, being the decisive event in all history, nothing that can ever happen will equal it in importance.

Jean Danielou

The death of Christ is the one truly revolutionary event that ever happened in the world.

W.G. Peck

It is Christ that died, yea rather, that is risen again, who is even at the right hand of God, who also maketh intercession for us.

Romans 8:34

Life doesn't begin at forty, or at twenty but at Calvary.

Elaine Kilgore

It is on the unshakable fact of the resurrection of Christ from the dead that I base my faith in God's utter integrity and faithfulness. He let Jesus die—but only because he would raise him again. You can count on him! You can stake your faith on God—the God of Jesus Christ. He will keep his word.

Leighton Ford

The resurrection is an incomprehensible event because it represents the inbreak of the eternal world of God into our temporal sphere.

Emil Brunner

The entire character of a man's whole life depends on whether he answers "Yes" or "No" to the historic fact of the Resurrection.

John E. Large

The knowledge of the ever-present Christ can reach down into the hidden depths and assure lonely modern man that he is not alone. More than that; it can draw him out of his loneliness to the rediscovery of the human race.

Stephen Neill

The Lord's Resurrection is not an isolated fact, it is a fact that concerns the whole of mankind; from Christ it extends to the world; it has a cosmic importance. . .the source of meaning to the human drama, the solution of the problem of evil, the origin of a new form of life, to which we give the name of Christianity.

Pope Paul VI

The resurrection of Jesus stands fast as a fact, unaffected by the waves of skepticism that ceaselessly through the ages beat themselves against it. It holds within it the vastest hope for time and eternity that humanity can ever know.

James Orr

It is on the reality of Christ's Resurrection that the religion that takes its name and life from him is founded.

Pope Paul VI

Without the Resurrection, Good Friday would only be the triumph of evil.

Maurice Nedoncelle

What did Resurrection mean but victory over death and therefore victory over sin and therefore the evidence of a new power at work in the world and therefore the opening of the gates of a new life?

Edwin Lewis

In the bonds of Death He lay
  Who for our defence was slain;
But the Lord is risen to-day.
  Christ hath brought us life again,
Wherefore let us all rejoice,
Singing loud, with cheerful voice,
  Hallelujah!

Martin Luther

Jesus was born twice. The birth at Bethlehem was a birth into a life of weakness. The second time he was born from the grave—"the first-born from the dead"—into the glory of heaven and the throne of God.

Andrew Murray

In Jesus and the primitive Church the prophetic spirit rose from the dead.

Walter Rauschenbusch

The Cross is where history and life, legend and reality, time and eternity intersect. There, Jesus is nailed for ever to show us how God could become a man and a man become God.

Malcolm Muggeridge

Blessed be the God and Father of our Lord Jesus Christ, which according to his abundant mercy hath begotten us again unto a lively hope by the resurrection of Jesus Christ from the dead, to an inheritance incorruptible, and undefiled, and that fadeth not away, reserved in heaven for you.

1 Peter 1:3, 4

One item about the resurrection of Jesus has sometimes been overlooked; he showed himself after death only to those who loved him.

George A. Buttrick

Certain it is that we are saved not by one cross but by two—Christ's and our own. We must be crucified with Christ, must die with him, and rise with him into a new way of life and being.

Arthur John Gossip

Reward

There is a reward for the obedient disciple, there are power and authority for the faithful disciple, there is glory of achievement for the zealous disciple; but there is the whisper of his love, the joy of his presence, and the shining of his face, for those who love Jesus for himself alone.

Susan B. Strachan

The big end of the branch is always toward the vine. The fruit comes on the little end. When we daily direct the big end of our lives toward Christ and his Word, an amazing thing takes place. The fruit comes on the little end. It will come in a way that will let us know that it was because of him and in spite of us.

Lane Adams

Let us with a gladsome mind
  Praise the Lord, for He is kind:
For His mercies aye endure,
  Ever faithful, ever sure.

All things living He doth feed;
  His full hand supplies their need:
For His mercies aye endure,
  Ever faithful, ever sure.

John Milton

Rest of the weary,
Joy of the sad,
Hope of the dreary,
Light of the glad,
Home of the stranger,
Strength to the end,
Refuge from danger,
Saviour and Friend!

John Samuel Bewley Monsell

My song is love unknown;
My Saviour's love to me;
Love to the loveless shown;
That they might lovely be
O, who am I,
That for my sake
My Lord should take
Frail fresh and die?

Samuel Crossman

To be thankful for what I have received, and for what my Lord has prepared, is the surest way to receive more.

Andrew Murray

Christ is rich, who will maintain you: He is a king, who will provide you: He is a sumptuous entertainer, who will feast you: He is beautiful, who will give in abundance all that can make you happy.

Edmund Campion

Jesus Christ can put joy into the joyless work of the twentieth century.

Bernard Ramm

They that deny themselves for Christ shall enjoy themselves in Christ.

John Mason

Above all the grace and the gifts that Christ gives to His beloved is that of overcoming self.

St. Francis of Assisi

He is a path, if any be misled;
  He is a robe, if any naked be;
If any chance to hunger, he is bread;
  If any be a bondman, he is free;
  If any be but weak, how strong is he!
To dead men life is he, to sick men health;
To blind men sight, and to the needy wealth;
A pleasure without loss, a treasure without stealth.

Giles Fletcher

For as the devil through pride led man from pride to death, so Christ through lowliness led back man through obedience to life.

St. Augustine of Hippo

Christian morality is the safe road from childhood to manhood, and the qualities enjoined by Jesus are indispensable to success in life.

Henry Ward Beecher

The Lord is my shepherd; I shall not want.

Psalm 23:1

Although Christ always remains the same in Himself, nevertheless the vision of Him that you see is not always of equal efficacy, but is patterned by the merits of the individuals whom He looks upon; into some He strikes, to others He brings comfort.

St. Gregory of Nyssa

In all the history of Christianity, whenever there has been a new emphasis upon Jesus, there has been a fresh outburst of vitality and virility.

E. Stanley Jones

Jesus threw a dam across the desert canyon of my life and brought in living water. The arid cracks filled up, the desert blossomed, and now he controls the outflow.

Carol Rhodes

Jesus Christ bought the controlling interest in my family business of Self & Co. He has brought stability to the firm. He has a gift for dealing with personnel problems and takes an optimistic view of future projects.

Alex Beale

I gave up all for Christ, and what have I found?
I have found everything in Christ!

John Calvin

One there is, above all others,
Well deserves the name of Friend;
His is love beyond a brother's,
Costly, free, and knows no end;
They who once His kindness prove
Find it everlasting love.

John Newton

The Lord is faithful, who shall stablish you, and keep you from evil.

2 Thessalonians 3:3

Christ is the best husband.

St. Augustine of Hippo

Faith is the Christian's foundation, hope is his anchor, death is his harbor, Christ is his pilot, and heaven is his country.

Jeremy Taylor

I laid at Christ's feet a self of which I was shamed, couldn't control, and couldn't live with; and to my glad astonishment he took that self, remade it, consecrated it to Kingdom purposes, and gave it back to me, a self I can now live with gladly and joyously and comfortably.

E. Stanley Jones

This for me will be the goal attained which has been for so long before my soul: I shall be so completely identified with him who has won my heart to himself, that I shall be like him forever, and with him through all the ages to come.

H.A. Ironside

Jesus promised his disciples three things: that they would be completely fearless, absurdly happy, and in constant trouble.

F.R. Maltby

To those who fall, how kind Thou art;
How good to those who seek;
But what to those who find? Ah, this
Nor tongue nor pen can show:
The love of Jesus, what it is,
None but His loved ones know.

St. Bernard of Clairvaux

Jesus Christ opens wide the doors of the treasure-house of God's promises, and bids us go in and take with boldness the riches that are ours.

Corrie Ten Boom

He loves each one of us, as if there were only one of us.

St. Augustine of Hippo

You must learn to make evils your great good and to spin comforts, peace, joy, communion with Christ, out of your troubles. They are Christ's wooers, sent to speak on your behalf to himself.

Samuel Rutherford

May His Counsels Sweet uphold you,
And His Loving Arms enfold you,
As you journey on your day.

May His Sheltering Wings protect you,
And His Light Divine direct you,
Turning darkness into day.

May His Potent Peace surround you,
And His Presence linger with you,
As your inner, golden ray.

Anonymous

S

SACRIFICE
SALVATION
SERVICE
SON OF MAN

Sacrifice

Jesus was the neighbor to the thief on the cross. That is, He was conscious of his need and did something about it. Imagine, even with His last breath of life almost gone, He gave to the dying thief.

James W. Kennedy

(Jesus), a man who was completely innocent, offered himself as a sacrifice for the good of others, including his enemies, and became the ransom of the world.

Ghandi

God commendeth his love toward us, in that, while we were yet sinners, Christ died for us.

Romans 5:8

Jesus Christ never met an unimportant person. That is why God sent his Son to die for us. If someone dies for you, you must be important.

M.C. Cleveland

The man, the Christ, the soldier,
Who from his cross of pain
Cried to the dying comrade,
"Lad, we shall meet again!"

Willard Wattles

The question remains, "How can God be just—that is, true to himself in nature and true to himself in holiness, and yet justify the sinner?" The only solution was for an innocent party to volunteer to die physically and spiritually as a substitution before God. There was only one possibility. God's own Son was the only personality in the universe who had the capacity to bear in his own body the sins of the world.

Billy Graham

The uniqueness of Jesus in the eyes of mankind is derived from a certain absoluteness of contrast between Him and the secular order within which He lived; and that contrast comes to its climax upon the Cross.

R. Roberts

When Jesus came to Golgotha,
  They hanged him on a tree,
They drove great nails through hands and feet,
  And made a Calvary;
They crowned him with a crown of thorns,
  Red were his wounds and deep,
For those were crude and cruel days,
  And human flesh was cheap.

G.A. Studdert-Kennedy

Suffering inflicted on Jesus by others had the appearance at least of being involuntary. The suffering of Gethsemane deep in his soul, could touch him only because he willed it, to give us courage in our own fears, to set us an example, to merit for us the grace needed in our own interior conflicts.

Ralph Gorman

It was in this submission of Himself, in which His human will was at one with His divine will, that Christ in His human life realized the perfection of Holiness: for Christ was not less holy on earth than He now is in heaven.

St. Cuthbert

And the Lord hath laid on him the iniquity of us all.

Isaiah 53:6

The death on the Cross—was the supreme witnessing act in His witnessing to the iniquity of sin against a world in which malice or ignorance would justify sin.

St. Cuthbert

The message of the Gospel is that in some true sense Christ died, not for general justice, but for me.

Willingston Walker

Jesus' Mission can be described as being twofold: it is a battle against the demons, and it is a battle for men. . . . Anybody who would understand history must be in possession of the category of the demonic.

Helmut Thielicke

Jesus Christ stoops and lets the sinner jump on His back, and so saves him from death.

Martin Luther

Whosoever would fully and feelingly understand the words of Christ, must endeavor to conform his life wholly to the life of Christ. . . . If thou seekest Jesus in all things, thou shalt surely find Jesus. . . . Set thyself therefore, like a good and faithful servant of Christ, to bear manfully the Cross of thy Lord Who out of love was crucified for thee.

Thomas à Kempis

For ye know the grace of our Lord Jesus Christ, that, though he was rich, yet for your sakes he became poor, that ye through his poverty might be rich.

2 Corinthians 8:9

The first lesson in Christ's school is self-denial.

Matthew Henri

Jesus hath many lovers of his Kingdom, but few bearers of His cross. All are disposed to rejoice with Him, but few suffer sorrow for His sake. Many follow Him to the breaking of the bread, but few to the drinking of His bitter cup.

Thomas à Kempis

He was born deserted, He lived alone, He died a lonely criminal's death; and if we want a proof that He felt it, we have it, first, in His frequent cries of pain, and second, in the eager way He grasped at and rewarded every mark of companionship offered Him.

Alban Goodier

If Christ has to be made perfect by suffering, much more must we. If He needed to learn obedience by sorrow, much more must we. If He needed in the days of His flesh, to make supplications to God His Father with strong crying and tears, so do we.

Charles Kingsley

We always find that those who walked closest to Christ Our Lord were those who had to bear the greatest trials.

St. Teresa of Avila

If you take that crabbed tree (the cross) and carry it lovingly, it will become to you like wings to a bird and sails of a ship.

Samuel Rutherford

In the cross of Christ excess in men is met by excess in God; excess of evil is mastered by excess of love.

Louis Bourdaloue

For the sake of each of us he laid down his life—worth no less than the universe. He demands of us in return our lives for the sake of each other.

St. Clement of Alexandria

If, when ye do well, and suffer for it, ye take it patiently, this is acceptable with God. For even hereunto were ye called: because Christ also suffered for us, leaving us an example, that ye should follow his steps.

1 Peter 2:20, 21

Jesus deliberately chooses the way of love, mercy, peace, and healing. Jesus chooses the way of nonviolence to overcome the violence of sin and death. Jesus chooses to be the sacrificial lamb, bearing our infirmities, enduring our sufferings, being crushed for our sins (see Isaiah 53:4, 5) so that he can take away the sin of the world.

Daniel Durken

I should give a false impression of my own convictions if I did not (state) that there is no hope of establishing a more Christian social order except through the labor and sacrifice of those in whom the Spirit of Christ is active.

William Temple

At the supreme moment of his dying Jesus so identified himself with men and the depths of their predicament and agony that no man can now sink so low that God has not gone lower.

Os Guinness

It was not weakness which made Christ hang on the Cross; it was obedience to the law of sacrifice, of love. For how could He save us if He ever saved Himself?

Fulton J. Sheen

No man took His life; He laid it down of Himself.

Robert Hugh Benson

The cross has revealed to good men that their goodness has not been good enough.

Johann Heronymus Schroeder

Salvation

It seemed so strange that on such slender thread as the feeble throb of an infant life the salvation of the world should hang—and no special care watch over its safety, no better shelter be provided it than a "stable," no other cradle than a manger! And it is still true. On what slender thread has the continued life of the church often seemed to hang! On what feeble throbbing that of every child of God—with no visible outward means to ward off danger, no home of comfort, no rest of ease.

Alfred Edersheim

Christ is the world's Redeemer,
The lover of the pure,
The fount of heavenly wisdom,
Our trust and hope secure;
The armour of His soldiers,
The Lord of earth and sky;
Our health while we are living,
Our life when we shall die.

St. Columba

The truth is, it is not Jesus as historically known, but Jesus as spiritually arisen within men, that is significant for our time, and can help it.

Albert Schweitzer

I call the attention of you young people to Jesus, the greatest leader, the most proficient teacher, the most absolutely right person the world has ever known. I tell you that the only way this world can be saved is by Jesus.

William Lyon Phelps

The Shepherds did not go to Bethlehem seeking the birth of a great man, or a famous teacher, or a national hero. They were promised a Savior.

Handel H. Brown

By a carpenter mankind was made, and only by that Carpenter can mankind be remade.

Desiderius Erasmus

The hands of Christ seem very frail,
For they were broken by a nail.
But only they reach Heaven at last
Whom these frail, broken hands hold fast.

John Richard Moreland

Our hope lies not in the man we put on the moon, but in the Man we put on the cross.

Dan Basham

The humility of Christ is the medicine of man's swollen pride.

St. Augustine of Hippo

If Christ had been too proud to die, he could not have helped us whose basic sin is pride. So Paul and others argue that by giving himself up without pride, Christ makes up for Adam's sin of arrogance. If all this is true, it comprises certainly the most momentous fact of human existence. Christ the free therapist for humanity, bringing us salvation as a gift of grace—that indeed is a daring postulate.

Rollo May

We moderns with all our pride in our boasted civilization are back where that ancient world was when it first confronted Christ. We are desperately in need of salvation. It is a humiliating experience for an individual or a whole generation to have to acknowledge that it needs to be saved, but only a blind man can fail to see that that is our situation now.

Harry Emerson Fosdick

None but the God we see in Jesus Christ will meet men's case.

Arthur John Gossip

The mission of Jesus cannot be defined without speaking of man being lost.

Henri Blocher

Sin is the disease. Christ the cure. The result is a miracle.

Frank Buchman

Jesus did not hang on the cross on his own account, but as our Representative. It was our death. . . . By his death he paid the wages of sin for us. . . . There is no longer any cause for anxiety except in the case of those who refuse to acknowledge their sinfulness, and turn their backs on the Man of Sorrows on the cross. We are delivered. . . . Whatever confusion and desolation may yet come upon our world, its future is secure.

F.W. Krummacher

He bent over the corpse of the dead world, and whispered a word of faith. . .uttered words then unknown,—love, sacrifice, a heavenly origin. And the dead arose. A new life circulated through the clay, which philosophy had tried in vain to reanimate.

Joseph Mazzini

For God so loved the world, that he gave his only begotten Son, that whosoever believeth in him should not perish, but have everlasting life. For God sent not his Son into the world to condemn the world; but that the world through him might be saved.

John 3:16, 17

I have taken much pains to know everything that is esteemed worth knowing among men; but with all my reading, nothing now remains to comfort me at the close of this life but this passage of the Apostole Paul: "It is a faithful saying, and worthy of all acceptation; that Jesus Christ came into the world to save sinners." To this I cleave, and herein do I find rest.

John Selden

The Holy walk, the devoted life of our Lord Jesus Christ could not avail to put away sin. It was life poured out in death that saved. Apart from his death, his life could only bring out in bold relief our exceeding sinfulness. But his blood shed for us was life given up, poured out in death that we might live eternally.

H.A. Ironside

As Man Alone, Jesus could not have saved us; as God alone, he would not; Incarnate, he could and did.

Malcolm Muggeridge

Though he were a Son, yet learned he obedience by the things which he suffered; and being made perfect, he became the author of eternal salvation unto all them that obey him.

Hebrews 5:8, 9

Neither is there salvation in any other: for there is none other name under heaven given among men, whereby we must be saved.

Acts 4:12

If thou shalt confess with thy mouth the Lord Jesus, and shalt believe in thine heart that God hath raised him from the dead, thou shalt be saved. For with the heart man believeth unto righteousness; and with the mouth confession is made unto salvation.

Romans 10:9, 10

There is one thing most of us forget. Christ taught it. The Church teaches it . . . though you wouldn't think so to hear a great many of us today. No one in good faith can ever be lost.

Archibald J. Cronin

He who does not himself remember that God redeemed him from sin and death by the life and passion of Jesus of Nazareth ceases to be a Christian.

Paul Ramsey

Whom [Jesus Christ] having not seen, ye love; in whom, though now ye see him not, yet believing, ye rejoice with joy unspeakable and full of glory: receiving the end of your faith, even the salvation of your souls.

1 Peter 1:8, 9

He said not,
  "Thou shalt not be
  Tempested;
Thou shalt not be
  Travailed;
Thou shalt not be
  Afflicted;
But he said,
  "Thou shalt not be
  Overcome!"

Julian of Norwick

The very act of faith by which we receive Christ is an act of utter renunciation of self and all its works, as a ground of salvation.

Mark Hopkins

In our scientific age there are thousands living who owe their lives to blood transfusions. By analogy, it can be reverently said that, in a mystical sense, the Son of God is the great universal Donor, giving new life to the sinner who trusts his shed blood for cleansing.

L. Nelson Bell

Believe on the Lord Jesus Christ, and thou shalt be saved, and thy house.

Acts 16:31

I should be ashamed to acknowledge him as my Savior if I could comprehend him—he would be no greater than I. Such is my sense of sin, and consciousness of my inability to save myself, that I feel I need a superhuman Savior.

Noah Webster

We do not receive things by prayer. We receive them by Jesus.

Armin Gesswein

I am crucified with Christ: nevertheless I live; yet not I, but Christ liveth in me: and the life which I now live in the flesh I live by the faith of the Son of God, who loved me, and gave himself for me.

Galatians 2:20

I am conscious that for me my only hope of salvation in this world lies in Christ.

Wilfred T. Grenfell

I stand before my neighbors on my character; but in heaven I have no standing myself at all. I stand there in the character of my Savior.

Paul Rader

Our Saviour Jesus Christ . . . hath abolished death, and hath brought life and immortality to light through the gospel.

2 Timothy 1:10

Service

Christ never was in a hurry. There was no rushing forward, no anticipating, no fretting over what might be. Each day's duties were done as each day brought them, and the rest was left with God.

Mary Slessor

The Lord Jesus Christ is the perfect example for all his followers, for he said, "I am among you as he that serves."

Philip E. Howard, Jr.

There was in Him no world-weariness, no strengthless melancholy, no timid shrinking from the fray.

Karl Adam

Thus has the Lord been teaching me to live upon myself not upon anything received from him but upon the Life itself.

Isaac Pennington

Our Lord does not care so much for the importance of our works as for the love with which they are done.

St. Teresa of Avila

The right practical divinity is this: Believe in Christ, and do your duty in that state of life to which God has called you.

Martin Luther

The task of life is not to be engaged in perpetual rebellion, but to find and serve our true Master.

E.L. Allen

What makes Christ's teachings difficult is that they obligate us to do something about them.

John J. Wade

All the faithful, without exception, are members of the mystical body of Jesus Christ. . . . All are therefore held, and today quite especially, to think, in prayer and sacrifice, not only of their own private needs, but also about the great intentions of the Kingdom of God in the world.

Pope Pius XII

The greatest competitor of devotion to Jesus is service for him.

Oswald Chambers

It is possible to be so active in the service of Christ as to forget to love him.

Peter T. Forsyth

The one thing that makes me even the kind of Christian that I am is that I dare not turn my back on Christ and put Him out of my life.

James Denney

The way of Christ is not possible without Christ.

William Russell Maltby

You cannot have Christian principles without Christ.

Dorothy L. Sayers

Jesus was not merely selfless; he was without self. He came "not to be ministered unto, but to minister," Jesus was selfless and therefore he was restful, because an adjustment to life that asks nothing for self always brings that happy result.

G.H. Morling

Of myself I can only say that I am an unprofitable servant; but I serve a good Master.

Richard Rothe

If we are one body to one Head—to Christ—then how shall we tolerate the presence amongst us of poor, hungry brothers?

Alexander Yelchaninov

In Jesus the service of God and the service of the least of the brethren were one.

Dietrich Bonhoeffer

And Jesus went about all Galilee, teaching in their synagogues, and preaching the gospel of the kingdom, and healing all manner of sickness and all manner of disease among the people.

Matthew 4:23

Soldiers of Christ! arise,
And put your armour on,
Strong in the strength which God supplies
Through His eternal Son;
Strong in the Lord of hosts,
And in His mighty power;
Who in the strength of Jesus trusts
Is more than conqueror.

Charles Wesley

He went about, he was so kind,
To cure poor people who were blind;
And many who were sick and lame,
He pitied them and did the same.

Ann and Jane Taylor

When he saw the multitudes, he was moved with compassion on them, because they fainted, and were scattered abroad, as sheep having no shepherd.

Matthew 9:36

He shall feed his flock like a shepherd.

Isaiah 40:11

Why should the Queen have good soldiers and not the King of Kings?

Mary Slessor

It is a tragedy when the mind, soul and heart are in slavery in a way of life which refuses to recognize that people have rights before God. It is a war which makes hate a badge of honor, slavery the keystone to prosperity. Not to resist would make one an accomplice to crime. Resistance was part of the program of Jesus. We must resist oppression and tyranny. We have to end it no matter what it costs.

Joseph R. Sizoo

The supreme need of the church is the same in the twentieth century as in the first; it is men on fire for Christ.

James S. Stewart

The sinner holds out a hand to the saint, gives a hand to the saint, since the saint gives a hand to the sinner. And all together, one by means of the other, one pulling up the other, they ascend to Jesus.

Charles Peguy

The Lord fishes on the bottom, and if you want to get to his bait and hook, brother, you've got to get right down on the bottom.

Sam Jones

Jesus Christ the transformer took my bundle of spiritual barbed-wire and electrified it into a high-voltage power line.

Yvonne Lehman

The demeanor, bearing and attitude of Jesus united . . . to arouse in others expectation and assurance of obtaining aid. . . . He ministered to people as he found them, touched life at every point, became the torchbearer of the bewildered. Small wonder that people had confidence in the one who had such a masterful spirit.

Karl Ruf Stolz

Even as the Son of man came not to be ministered unto, but to minister, and to give his life a ransom for many.

Matthew 20:28

One of the most amazing things ever said on this earth is Jesus's statement: "He that is greatest among you shall be your servant." Nobody has one chance in a billion of being thought really great after a century has passed except those who have been the servants of all. That strange realist from Bethlehem knew that.

Harry Emerson Fosdick

We are all making a crown for Jesus out of these daily lives of ours, either a crown of golden, divine love, studded with gems of sacrifice and adoration, or a thorny crown, filled with the cruel briars of unbelief, or selfishness, and sin, and placing it upon His brow.

Aimee Semple McPherson

Our confidence in Christ does not make us lazy, negligent, or careless, but on the contrary it awakens us, urges us on, and makes us active in living righteous lives and doing good. There is no self-confidence to compare with this.

Ulrich Zwingli

O, Jesus, I have promised
To serve Thee to the end;
Be Thou for ever near me,
My Master and my Friend:
I shall not fear the battle
If Thou art by my side,
Nor wander from the pathway
If Thou wilt be my guide.

John Ernest Bode

Though we do not have our Lord with us in bodily presence, we have our neighbor, who, for the ends of love and loving service, is as good as our Lord himself.

St. Teresa of Avila

Son of Man

Jesus of the Gospels is the contrary of an artificial and composite being. Here is the most moving of the great figures of history, and of all the great characters history places before us, the least logical because he is the most living.

François Mauriac

The most profound tendencies of Luther's thoughts show that in the human words and works of Jesus, God is revealed. . . . He had from the beginning thought of the two natures of Christ as so united that the man Jesus was, in all the words and works, the expression and organ of his divine nature. He knew no God except the One revealed in the man Jesus.

Reinhold Seeberg

Christ is God clothed with human nature.

Benjamin Whichcote

Jesus is the true prototype of the human race.

Christoph Ernst Luthardt

Trumpets! Lightnings! The earth trembles!
But into the Virgin's womb thou didst descend with noiseless tread.

Agathias Scholasticus

What manner of man is this, that even the winds and the sea obey him!

Matthew 8:27

He proclaimed that to gain the whole world was nothing if the soul were injured, and yet he remained kind and sympathetic to every living thing. That is the most astonishing, and the greatest fact about him!

Adolf Von Harnack

There was something that He hid from all men when He went up a mountain to pray. There was something He covered constantly by abrupt silence or impetuous isolation. There was some one thing that was too great for God to show us when He walked upon our earth; and I have sometimes fancied that it was His mirth.

Gilbert K. Chesterton

The most fascinating figure in history. In him is combined what is best and most mysterious and most enchanting in Israel—the eternal people whose child he was.

Hyman G. Enelow

He is unique, He transcends all the known frontiers and boundaries. He shares in many of the ideas and in the outlooks and expectations of the time. But he is always far beyond them.

Rufus M. Jones

Jesus Christ was perfectly human precisely because his human nature was in unfailing communion with the Divine Nature. He was not less a man, but more a man, because He was also God.

Gerald Groveland Walsh

In him, as in no other, God lived; he lived, as no other ever did, in God. Since Jesus lived, God has been another and nearer Being to man.

Andrew M. Fairbairn

(To an educated Hindu) Jesus is a supreme illustration of the growth from human origins to divine destiny. . . . He is the great hero who exemplifies the noblest characteristics of manhood, the revealer of the profoundest depths in ourselves, one who brings home to us the ideal of human perfection by embodying it in himself.

Radhakrishnan

The Lord from Heaven,
Born of a village girl, carpenter's son
Wonderful, Prince of Peace, the mighty God.

Alfred Lord Tennyson

The best of men
That e'er wore earth about him was a sufferer;
A soft, meek, patient, humble, tranquil spirit,
The first true gentleman that ever breathed.

Thomas Dekker

Jesus Christ alone stands at the absolute center of humanity, the one completed harmonious man. He is the absolute and perfect truth, the highest that humanity can reach; at once its perfect image and supreme Lord.

Charles W. French

Christ, if we call him a philosopher . . . was the poor man's philosopher, the first and only one that has appeared.

Horace Bushell

Whatever other philosophers may have been, he alone is a teacher from heaven; he alone was able to teach certain and eternal wisdom; he alone taught things pertaining to our salvation, because he alone is its author; he alone absolutely practiced what he preached, and is able to make good what he promised.

Desiderius Erasmus

Christ, who expresses both the infinite possibilities of love in human life and the infinite possibilities beyond human life, is . . . a true revelation of the total situation in which human life stands.

Reinhold Niebuhr

What Christ brought to light in the unfolding of the Eternal Gospel is the Face, the personal aspect, the revelation of the Heart, the Love, the Grace, the Character-Nature of God. We see Him at last.

Rufus M. Jones

The most scientific man that ever trod the globe. He plunged beneath the material surface of things, and found the spiritual cause.

Mary Baker Eddy

God is to me that creative Force, behind and in the universe, who manifests Himself as energy, as life, as order, as beauty, as thought, as conscience, as love, and who is self-revealed supremely in the creative Person of Jesus of Nazareth.

William Sloane Coffin

As all the sweetness that is in the flowers of the field and in the garden is brought by the bees into the hive, and is there embodied in one hive; so all the attributes of God and the sweetness of them are hived in Christ, in whom all the fullness of the Godhead dwells bodily.

William Bridge

The immanent Spiritual Life of God focalized in a human personality.

Shailer Mathews

Christ came in human form chiefly for the purpose of awakening man to a sense of divine possibilities.

Joseph McSorley

He was the personal embodiment of truths which are permanently central for the spiritual life of mankind.

Eugene W. Lyman

If asked what precisely is the distinctive feature in the ethics of Christ, I should be inclined to answer, "The fact that it is not ethics at all.". . . Christ, instead of a code, gives an ideal; instead of rules, a life; instead of a philosophy, an art.

Burnett H. Streeter

In considering the teachings of Jesus as a whole, we find that he was the Oriental of the Orientals. He was the ideal of typical Oriental life. In other words he was the embodiment of the ideals the Oriental people cherished and manifested in their thought and actions.

Swami Akhilananda

We can hardly think of Jesus Christ without thinking of the sparrows, the grass, fig-trees, sheep.

Vincent McNabb

T

TEMPTATION

TRANQUILLITY

Temptation

We shall never understand anything of our Lord's preaching and ministry unless we continually keep in mind what exactly and exclusively his errand was in this world. Sin was his errand in this world, and it was his only errand. He would never have been in this world, either preaching or doing anything else, but for sin. He could have done everything else for us without coming down into this world at all; everything else but take away our sin.

Alexander Whyte

Christ didn't waste His time trying to change the social order. Christ spent all His time fighting sin. Therefore it behooves the witnesses of Christ to say that we do not have to abolish capitalism and establish socialism or communism, that sin can flourish under those systems as well, Christianity is not opposed to any social order, but to sin.

John H. McComb

Don't try to deal with sin, for you are sure to lose. Deal with Christ; let him deal with your sin and you are sure to win.

Arthur H. Elfstrand

If we try to look away from the name of Jesus Christ even momentarily, the Christian Church loses the substance in virtue of which it can assert itself in and against the State and society as an entity of a special order.

Karl Barth

Jesus Christ himself is the Way. If we have gone astray from the Way, it is because we have strayed from Jesus Christ. It is not just doctrine about him, or knowledge of him, or experience of the blessings he can give: it is his own living Presence which is the Way.

Wesley W. Nelson

Jesus knew that he had come to kindle a fire on earth. . . . He saw that what was exalted among man was an abomination before God.

Walter Rauschenbusch

If we assume the words of Christ to have meant the very least that they could mean, His words must at the very least mean this—that rich men are not very likely to be morally trustworthy.

Gilbert K. Chesterton

To ask the individual to follow Christ in much of the business world today is almost like asking a man to live Christ while employed in a gambling house.

Jerome Davis

Any unmortified desire which a man allows in will effectually drive and keep Christ out of the heart.

Charles Wesley

God harden me against myself,
This coward with pathetic voice
Who craves for ease, and rest, and joys:
Myself, arch-traitor to myself;
My hollowest friend, my deadliest foe,
My clog whatever road I go.
Yet One there is can curb myself,
Can roll the strangling load from me,
Break off the yoke and set me free.

Christina Rossetti

I could give no reply except a lazy and drowsy, "Yes, Lord, yes. I'll get to it right away; just don't bother me for a little while." But "right away" didn't happen right away; and "a little while" turned out to be a very long while.

St. Augustine of Hippo

Sun of my soul, Thou Saviour dear,
It is not night if Thou be near;
O may no earth-born cloud arise
To hide Thee from Thy servant's eyes.

John Keble

When I came to believe in Christ's teaching, I ceased desiring what I had wished for before. The direction of my life, my desires, became different. What was good and bad changed places.

Leo Tolstoy

Hell was not prepared for man. God never meant that man would ever go to hell. Hell was prepared for the devil and his angels, but man rebelled against God and followed the devil. . . . Hell is essentially and basically banishment from the presence of God for deliberately rejecting Jesus Christ as Lord and Savior.

Billy Graham

Tranquillity

Jesus, Deliverer,
Come Thou to me;
Soothe Thou my voyaging
Over life's sea:
Thou, when the storm of death
Roars, sweeping by,
Whisper, O Truth of Truth,
'Peace! It is I.'

Eighteenth-century hymn

All his glory and beauty come from within, and there He delights to dwell, His visits there are frequent, His conversation sweet, His comfort refreshing; and His peace passing all understanding.

Thomas à Kempis

Above all, I try to avoid the temptation to which anyone who speaks to heathens is subject, to "preach the law." It is difficult not to cite the Ten Commandments and thus prepare for the gospel people to whom lying, stealing and immorality are second nature. I strive to awaken in their hearts the longing for peace with God. When I speak of the difference between the restless and the peaceful heart, the wildest of my savages knows what is meant. And when I portray Jesus as He who brings peace with God to the hearts of men, they comprehend Him.

Albert Schweitzer

Christ's life outwardly was one of the most troubled lives that was ever lived: tempest and tumult, tumult and tempest, the waves breaking over it all the time. But the inner life was a sea of glass. The great calm was always there.

Henry Drummond

The storm was raging. The sea was beating against the rocks in huge, dashing waves. The lightning was flashing, the thunder was roaring, the wind was blowing; but the little bird was sound asleep in the crevice of the rock, its head tucked serenely under its wing. That is peace, to be able to sleep in the storm! In Christ we are relaxed and at peace in the midst of the confusions, bewilderments and perplexities of this life. The storm rages, but our hearts are at rest. We have found peace—at last!

Billy Graham

The only way that we can solve the problem of aggression is the way that Jesus advocated: "Father, forgive them; for they know not what they do." Again it was said by Buddha: "If one man conquer in battle a thousand times thousand men, and if another conquer himself, he is the greatest of conquerors."

Swami Akhilananda

The calmness bends serene above
  My restlessness to still;
Around me flows Thy quickening Life,
  To nerve my faltering will;
Thy presence fills my solitude;
Thy province turns all to good.

Henry Wadsworth Longfellow

We are not a postwar generation, but a pre-peace generation. Jesus is coming.

Corrie Ten Boom

Know that our Lord is called in Scripture the Prince of Peace, and hence, wherever He is absolute Master, He preserves peace.

St. Francis of Sales

Blessed are the peacemakers: for they shall be called the children of God.

Matthew 5:9

O Lord, Jesus Christ, Who art as the Shadow of a Great Rock in a weary land, Who beholdest Thy weak creatures weary of labour, weary of pleasure, weary of hope deferred, weary of self; in Thine abundant compassion, and fellow feeling with us, and unutterable tenderness, bring us, we pray Thee, unto Thy rest.

Christina Rossetti

The peace of the spiritual Christian is that of Christ's presence. . . . The spiritual man lives habitually under the dominating control of the Holy Spirit who indwells him. . . . It is a life of winsome holiness.

Ruth Paxson

Are you looking unto Jesus now, in the immediate matter that is pressing, and receiving from him peace? If so, he will be a gracious benediction of peace in and through you. But if you try to worry it out, you obliterate him and deserve all you get.

Oswald Chambers

Be Thou our great Deliverer still,
Thou Lord of life and death;
Restore and quicken, soothe and bless,
With Thine almighty breath;
To hands that work and eyes that see
Give wisdom's heavenly lore,
That whole and sick, and weak and strong,
May praise Thee evermore.

Edward Hayes Plumptre

Jesus, the very thought of Thee
With sweetness fills my breast;
But sweeter far Thy face to see,
and in Thy presence rest.

St. Bernard of Clairvaux

The peace of God, which passeth all understanding, shall keep your hearts and minds through Christ Jesus.

Philippians 4:7

WORSHIP

Worship

No condemnation now I dread;
Jesus, and all in Him, is mine!
Alive in Him, my living Head,
And clothed in righteousness divine,
Bold I approach the eternal throne,
And claim the crown, through Christ my own.

Charles Wesley

The heart of a believer affected with the glory of Christ is like the needle touched with the lodestone. It can no longer be quiet, no longer be satisfied in a distance from Him.

John Owen

For we preach not ourselves, but Christ Jesus the Lord; and ourselves your servants for Jesus' sake.

2 Corinthians 4:5

To love him with all the heart, and with all the understanding, and with all the soul, and with all the strength, and to love his neighbor as himself, is more than all whole burnt offerings and sacrifices.

Mark 12:33

The moment I awaked, "Jesus, Master," was in my heart and in my mouth; and I found all my strength lay in keeping my eye fixed upon Him, and my soul waiting on Him continually.

John Wesley

The Church's one foundation is Jesus Christ her Lord;
She is His new creation by water and the Word.

Samuel John Stone

The truth of the Christian religion is in fact enclosed in the one name of Jesus Christ and nothing else.

Karl Barth

The orthodox Christian world has forgotten and forsaken the real, human Jesus of the Gospels, and has substituted a "Christ" of dogmatism, metaphysics, and pagan philosophy.

Karl M. Choworowsky

Where Christ is not the living center of everything the value of the Church has declined, its life has waned. That, to my mind, is the most striking and outstanding fact in history.

T.R. Glover

The Christian Church stands or falls with this simple proposition: that Jesus is nothing less than God's self-communication to man, and the only certain source of our knowledge of God.

W.A. Visser 'T Hooft

The historical Jesus has a different category of sins from that of the Old Testament or of Paul or of ecclesiastical writers after him. The sins which occupied the attention of Jesus were hypocrisy, worldliness, intolerance, and selfishness. The sins which occupy the principal attention of the Church . . . are impurity, murder, the drinking of alcohol, swearing, the neglect of the Church's services and ordinances.

Robert Keable

Since the time of Jesus there have been some advances in religion . . . but these advances are usually admitted to be nothing more than the explication of what was already implicit in the teaching of Jesus. We are still trying to catch up with Him.

D.E. Trueblood

The revivals and reforms of the Church have commonly been due to a sudden consciousness that Jesus Christ has been forgotten or undervalued in the very Church which bore His name.

James Moffat

In every decade we instruct Christ as to what He was and is, instead of allowing ourselves to be instructed by Him.

Amos N. Wilder

We need to forget the imaginary Christ who has been ours too long and to rediscover the real Christ, the Christ of the prophets and the martyrs and the confessors, the Christ who is not only the lover of souls but also the master, a monarch with demands to make in industry, in finance, in education, in the arts, in marriage, in the home.

Bernard Iddings Bell

We may say if we wish, that Christ is never found outside the Church, but we must add in the same breath that wherever Christ is, there is the Church.

Chad Waleh

Christ always lives where there is room for him. If there is room in your heart for Christ, he lives there; if there is room in a law office for Christ, he lives there; if there is room on a locomotive engine, he will be there; if there is room in a baggage car, he will be there.

Sam Jones

Being a Christian is more than just an instantaneous conversion—it is a daily process whereby you grow to be more and more like Christ. Jesus Christ is the man God wants every man to be like.

Billy Graham

Christ is with those of humble mind, not with those who exalt themselves over his flock.

St. Clement of Rome

Jesus taught, first, that a man's business is to do the will of God; second, that God takes upon himself the care of that man; third, therefore, that a man must never be afraid of anything; and so, fourth, be left free to love God with all his heart, and his neighbor as himself.

George Macdonald

And besides this, giving all diligence, add to your faith virtue; and to virtue, knowledge; and to knowledge, temperance; and to temperance, patience; and to patience, godliness; and to godliness, brotherly kindness; and to brotherly kindness, charity. For if these things be in you, and abound, they make you that ye shall neither be barren nor unfruitful in the knowledge of our Lord Jesus Christ.

2 Peter 1:5-8

The older I grow in years, the more the wonder and the joy increase when I see the power of these words of Jesus—"I have called you friends"—to move the human heart. That one word "friend" breaks down each barrier of reserve, and we have boldness in his presence. Our hearts go out in love to meet his love.

George F. Andrews

Thou art the Way; to Thee alone
From sin and death we flee;
And he who would the Father seek
Must seek Him, Lord, by Thee.

George Washington Doane

The religion of Christ is a mystery which subsists by its own force, and proceeds from a mind which is not a human mind.

Napoleon Bonaparte

A man who loves his wife will love her letters and her photographs because they speak to him of her. So if we love the Lord Jesus we shall love the Bible because it speaks to us of him.

John R.W. Scott

Seek ye the Lord while he may be found, call ye upon him while he is near.

Isaiah 55:6

If Shakespeare should come into this room, we would all rise; but if Jesus Christ should come in, we would all kneel.

Charles Lamb

Lord, who shall abide in thy tabernacle?
Who shall dwell in thy holy hill?

He that walketh uprightly, and
  worketh righteousness,
and speaketh the truth in his heart.

Psalm 15:1, 2

I have one passion only: It is He! It is He!

Nicholas Von Zindendorf

If you knew that there was One greater than yourself, who knows you better than you know yourself, and loves you better than you can love yourself; One who gathered into himself all great and good things and causes, blending in his beauty all the enduring color of life, who could turn your dreams into visions, and make real the things you hoped were true; and if that One had done one unmistakable thing to prove, even at the price of blood—his own blood—that you could come to him, would you not fall at his feet with the treasure of your years, your powers, your love? And is there not One such?

A.E. Whitham

We love him, because he first loved us.

1 John 4:19

The backbone of all moral attitudes is the love of God, through Christ, with Christ, and in Christ.

Dietrich Von Hildebrand

To be like Christ is to be a Christian.

William Penn

The test of worship is how far it makes us more sensitive to "the beyond in our midst," to the Christ in the hungry, the naked, the homeless and the prisoner.

J.A.T. Robinson

PART III

WHAT JESUS SAID

FAITH

FORGIVENESS

Faith

I am the true vine, and my Father is the husbandman. Every branch in me that beareth not fruit he taketh away: and every branch that beareth fruit, he purgeth it, that it may bring forth more fruit.

Abide in me, and I in you. As the branch cannot bear fruit of itself, except it abide in the vine; no more can ye, except ye abide in me.I am the vine, ye are the branches. He that abideth in me, and I in him, the same bringeth forth much fruit; for without me ye can do nothing.

John 15:1, 2, 4, 5

He that believeth and is baptized shall be saved; but he that believeth not shall be damned.

Mark 16:16

And these signs shall follow them that believe; In my name shall they cast out devils; they shall speak with new tongues.

Mark 16:17

Every man therefore that hath heard, and hath learned of the Father, cometh unto me.

John 6:45

Let not your heart be troubled: ye believe in God, believe also in me.

Peace I leave with you, my peace I give unto you: not as the world giveth, give I unto you. Let not your heart be troubled, neither let it be afraid.

John 14:1, 27

It is the Spirit that quickeneth; the flesh profiteth nothing: the words that I speak unto you, they are spirit, and they are life.

John 6:63

Though ye believe not me, believe the works; that ye may know, and believe, that the Father is in me, and I in him.

John 10:38

I have prayed for thee, that thy faith fail not.

Luke 22:32

Follow me, and I will make you fishers of men.

Matthew 4:19

Take therefore no thought for the morrow: for the morrow shall take thought for the things of itself. Sufficient unto the day is the evil thereof.

Matthew 6:34

Jesus saith unto her, Said I not unto thee, that, if thou wouldest believe, thou shouldest see the glory of God? Then they took away the stone from the place where the dead was laid. And Jesus lifted up his eyes, and said, Father, I thank thee that thou hast heard me. And I knew that thou hearest me always: but because of the people which stand by I said it, that they may believe that thou hast sent me. And when he thus had spoken, he cried with a loud voice, Lazarus, come forth. And he that was dead came forth, bound hand and foot with graveclothes; and his face was bound about with a napkin. Jesus saith unto them, Loose him, and let him go.

John 11:40-44

Beware of false prophets.

Matthew 7:15
(Sermon on the Mount)

He that believeth on me, the works that I do shall he do also; and greater works than these shall he do; because I go unto the Father.

John 14:12

Whosoever heareth these sayings of mine, and doeth them, I will liken him unto a wise man, which built his house upon a rock: and the rain descended, and the floods came, and the winds blew, and beat upon that house; and it fell not: for it was founded upon a rock.

Matthew 7:24, 25
(Sermon on the Mount)

Thomas, Reach hither thy finger, and behold my hands; and reach hither thy hand, and thrust it into my side; and be not faithless, but believing. . . .And Thomas answered and said unto him, My Lord and my God. Jesus saith unto him, Thomas, because thou hast seen me, thou hast believed: blessed are they that have not seen, and yet have believed.

John 20:27-29
(Doubting Thomas)

Thy faith hath saved thee; go in peace.

Luke 7:50

I am the light of the world.

John 8:12

Be thou faithful unto death, and I will give thee a crown of life.

Revelation 2:10

It is expedient for you that I go away: for if I go not away, the Comforter will not come unto you; but if I depart, I will send him unto you.

John 16:7

When the Comforter is come, whom I will send unto you from the Father, even the Spirit of truth, which proceedeth from the Father, he shall testify of me.

John 15:26

It is not for you to know the times or the seasons, which the Father hath put in his own power. But ye shall receive power, after that the Holy Ghost is come upon you: and ye shall be witnesses unto me both in Jerusalem, and in all Judea, and in Samaria, and unto the uttermost part of the earth.

Acts 1:7, 8

If any man thirst, let him come unto me, and drink.

John 7:37

Come unto me, all ye that labor and are heavy laden, and I will give you rest. Take my yoke upon you, and learn of me; for I am meek and lowly in heart: and ye shall find rest unto your souls. For my yoke is easy, and my burden is light.

Matthew 11:28-30

He that is not with me is against me; and he that gathereth not with me scattereth abroad.

Matthew 12:30

Man shall not live by bread alone, but by every word that proceedeth out of the mouth of God.

Matthew 4:4

The world cannot hate you; but me it hateth, because I testify of it, that the works thereof are evil.

John 7:7

Behold, I stand at the door, and knock: if any man hear my voice, and open the door, I will come in to him, and will sup with him, and he with me.

Revelation 3:20

I am the door: by me if any man enter in, he shall be saved, and shall go in and out, and find pasture.

John 10:9

Heaven and earth shall pass away, but my words shall not pass away.

Matthew 24:35

I am Alpha and Omega, the beginning and the end, the first and the last.

Revelation 22:13

Forgiveness

Ye have heard that it hath been said, An eye for an eye, and a tooth for a tooth: but I say unto you, That ye resist not evil: but whosoever shall smite thee on thy right cheek, turn to him the other also. And if any man will sue thee at the law, and take away thy coat, let him have thy cloak also. And whosoever shall compel thee to go a mile, go with him twain. Give to him that asketh thee, and from him that would borrow of thee turn not thou away.

Matthew 5:38-42
(Sermon on the Mount)

Judge not, that ye be not judged. For with what judgment ye judge, ye shall be judged: and with what measure ye mete, it shall be measured to you again. And why beholdest thou the mote that is in thy brother's eye, but considerest not the beam that is in thine own eye? Or how wilt thou say to thy brother, Let me pull out the mote out of thine eye; and, behold, a beam is in thine own eye? Thou hypocrite, first cast out the beam out of thine own eye; and then shalt thou see clearly to cast out the mote out of thy brother's eye.

Matthew 7:1-5
(Sermon on the Mount)

They that be whole need not a physician, but they that are sick. But go ye and learn what that meaneth, I will have mercy, and not sacrifice: for I am not come to call the righteous, but sinners to repentance.

Matthew 9:12, 13

Judge not, and ye shall not be judged: condemn not, and ye shall not be condemned: forgive, and ye shall be forgiven: give, and it shall be given unto you; good measure, pressed down, and shaken together, and running over, shall men give into your bosom. For with the same measure that ye mete withal it shall be measured to you again.

Luke 6:37, 38

For if ye forgive men their trespasses, your heavenly Father will also forgive you: but if ye forgive not men their trespasses, neither will your Father forgive your trespasses.

Matthew 6:14
(Sermon on the Mount)

I say unto you, All manner of sin and blasphemy shall be forgiven unto men: but the blasphemy against the Holy Ghost shall not be forgiven unto men. And whosoever speaketh a word against the Son of man, it shall be forgiven him: but whosoever speaketh against the Holy Ghost, it shall not be forgiven him, neither in this world, neither in the world to come.

Matthew 12:31, 32

If any man hear my words, and believe not, I judge him not: for I came not to judge the world, but to save the world. He that rejecteth me, and receiveth not my words, hath one that judgeth him: the word that I have spoken, the same shall judge him in the last day. For I have not spoken of myself; but the Father which sent me, he gave me a commandment, what I should say, and what I should speak.

John 12:47-49

How think ye? if a man have a hundred sheep, and one of them be gone astray, doth he not leave the ninety and nine, and goeth into the mountains, and seeketh that which is gone astray? And if so be that he find it, verily I say unto you, he rejoiceth more of that sheep, than of the ninety and nine which went not astray. Even so it is not the will of your Father which is in heaven, that one of these little ones should perish.

Matthew 18:12-14

If thy brother shall trespass against thee, go and tell him his fault between thee and him alone: if he shall hear thee, thou hast gained thy brother.

Matthew 18:15

Therefore is the kingdom of heaven likened unto a certain king, which would take account of his servants. And when he had begun to reckon, one was brought unto him, which owed him ten thousand talents. But forasmuch as he had not to pay, his lord commanded him to be sold, and his wife, and children, and all that he had, and payment to be made. The servant therefore fell down, and worshipped him, saying, Lord, have patience with me, and I will pay thee all. Then the lord of that servant was moved with compassion, and loosed him, and forgave him the debt.

Matthew 18:23-27
(Parable of the Merciful Debtor)

But I say unto you, That every idle word that men shall speak, they shall give account thereof in the day of judgment. For by thy words thou shalt be justified, and by thy words thou shalt be condemned.

Matthew 12:36, 37

Judge not according to the appearance, but judge righteous judgment.

John 7:24

Therefore if thou bring thy gift to the altar, and there rememberest that thy brother hath aught against thee; leave there thy gift before the altar, and go thy way; first be reconciled to thy brother, and then come and offer thy gift.

Matthew 5:23, 24

Seest thou this woman? I entered into thine house, thou gavest me no water for my feet: but she hath washed my feet with tears, and wiped them with the hairs of her head. Thou gavest me no kiss: but this woman, since the time I came in, hath not ceased to kiss my feet. My head with oil thou didst not anoint: but this woman hath anointed my feet with ointment. Wherefore I say unto thee, Her sins, which are many, are forgiven; for she loved much: but to whom little is forgiven, the same loveth little.

Luke 7:44-47

Now ye are clean through the word which I have spoken unto you.

John 15:3

Jesus answered, Neither hath this man sinned, nor his parents: but that the works of God should be made manifest in him.

John 9:3

Father, forgive them; for they know not what they do.

Luke 23:34

K

KINGDOM OF HEAVEN

Kingdom of Heaven

When the Son of man shall come in his glory, and all the holy angels with him, then shall he sit upon the throne of his glory: and before him shall be gathered all nations: and he shall separate them one from another, as a shepherd divideth his sheep from the goats: and he shall set the sheep on his right hand, but the goats on the left. Then shall the King say unto them on his right hand, Come, ye blessed of my Father, inherit the kingdom prepared for you from the foundation of the world: for I was ahungered, and ye gave me meat: I was thirsty, and ye gave me drink: I was a stranger, and ye took me in: naked, and ye clothed me: I was sick, and ye visited me: I was in prison, and ye came unto me. Then shall the righteous answer him, saying, Lord, when saw we thee ahungered, and fed thee? or thirsty, and gave thee drink? When saw we thee a stranger, and took thee in? or naked, and clothed thee? Or when saw we thee sick, or in prison, and came unto thee? And the King shall answer and say unto them, Verily I say unto you, Inasmuch as ye have done it unto one of the least of these my brethren, ye have done it unto me.

Matthew 25:31-40

Suffer the little children to come unto me, and forbid them not; for of such is the kingdom of God. Verily I say unto you, Whosoever shall not receive the kingdom of God as a little child, he shall not enter therein.

Mark 10:14, 15

Verily, verily, I say unto you, He that believeth on me hath everlasting life. I am that bread of life. Your fathers did eat manna in the wilderness, and are dead. This is the bread which cometh down from heaven, that a man may eat thereof, and not die. I am the living bread which came down from heaven: if any man eat of this bread, he shall live for ever: and the bread that I will give is my flesh, which I will give for the life of the world.

John 6:47-51

Verily, verily, I say unto you, Hereafter ye shall see heaven open, and the angels of God ascending and descending upon the Son of man.

John 1:51

When these things begin to come to pass, then look up, and lift up your heads; for your redemption draweth nigh.

Luke 21:28

Verily I say unto you, Except ye be converted, and become as little children, ye shall not enter into the kingdom of heaven. Whosoever therefore shall humble himself as this little child, the same is greatest in the kingdom of heaven.

Matthew 18:3, 4

I am the resurrection, and the life: he that believeth in me, though he were dead, yet shall he live.

John 11:25

All that the Father giveth me shall come to me; and him that cometh to me I will in no wise cast out. For I came down from heaven, not to do mine own will, but the will of him that sent me. And this is the Father's will which hath sent me, that of all which he hath given me I should lose nothing, but should raise it up again at the last day. And this is the will of him that sent me, that every one which seeth the Son, and believeth on him, may have everlasting life: and I will raise him up at the last day.

John 6:37-40

He that findeth his life shall lose it: and he that loseth his life for my sake shall find it.

Matthew 10:39

Think not that I am come to destroy the law, or the prophets: I am not come to destroy, but to fulfill. For verily I say unto you, Till heaven and earth pass, one jot or one tittle shall in no wise pass from the law, till all be fulfilled.

Matthew 5:17, 18
(Sermon on the Mount)

Ye have heard how I said unto you, I go away, and come again unto you.

John 14:28

And, lo, I am with you alway, even unto the end of the world.
Matthew 28:20

I will not leave you comfortless: I will come to you. Yet a little while, and the world seeth me no more; but ye see me: because I live, ye shall live also. At that day ye shall know that I am in my Father, and ye in me, and I in you.

John 14:18-20

If a man keep my saying, he shall never see death.

John 8:51

Thou art not far from the kingdom of God.

Mark 12:34

These things I have spoken unto you, that in me ye might have peace. In the world ye shall have tribulation: but be of good cheer; I have overcome the world.

John 16:33

There shall not a hair of your head perish.

Luke 21:18

Blessed are ye, when men shall revile you, and persecute you, and shall say all manner of evil against you falsely, for my sake. Rejoice, and be exceeding glad: for great is your reward in heaven.

Matthew 5:11, 12
(Sermon on the Mount—Beatitudes)

Again, the kingdom of heaven is like unto a net, that was cast into the sea, and gathered of every kind: which, when it was full, they drew to shore, and sat down, and gathered the good into vessels, but cast the bad away. So shall it be at the end of the world: the angels shall come forth, and sever the wicked from among the just, and shall cast them into the furnace of fire: there shall be wailing and gnashing of teeth.

Matthew 13:47-50

Verily, verily, I say unto you, He that heareth my word, and believeth on him that sent me, hath everlasting life, and shall not come into condemnation; but is passed from death unto life.

John 5:24

The hour is coming, and now is, when the dead shall hear the voice of the Son of God: and they that hear shall live.

John 5:25

My sheep hear my voice, and I know them, and they follow me: and I give unto them eternal life; and they shall never perish, neither shall any man pluck them out of my hand. My Father, which gave them me, is greater than all; and no man is able to pluck them out of my Father's hand. I and my Father are one.

John 10:27-30

Lay not up for yourselves treasures upon earth, where moth and rust doth corrupt, and where thieves break through and steal: but lay up for yourselves treasures in heaven, where neither moth nor rust doth corrupt, and where thieves do not break through nor steal: for where your treasure is, there will your heart be also.

Matthew 6:19-21
(Sermon on the Mount)

Seek ye first the kingdom of God, and his righteousness.

Matthew 6:33
(Sermon on the Mount)

For what is a man profited, if he shall gain the whole world, and lose his own soul? or what shall a man give in exchange for his soul? For the Son of man shall come in the glory of his Father with his angels; and then he shall reward each man according to his works.

Matthew 16:26, 27

How hardly shall they that have riches enter into the kingdom of God! For it is easier for a camel to go through a needle's eye, than for a rich man to enter into the kingdom of God.

Luke 18:24, 25

Fear not, little flock; for it is your Father's good pleasure to give you the kingdom. Sell that ye have, and give alms; provide yourselves bags which wax not old, a treasure in the heavens that faileth not, where no thief approacheth, neither moth corrupteth. For where your treasure is, there will your heart be also.

Luke 12:32-34

Seek not ye what ye shall eat, or what ye shall drink, neither be ye of doubtful mind. For all these things do the nations of the world seek after: and your Father knoweth that ye have need of these things. But rather seek ye the kingdom of God; and all these things shall be added unto you.

Luke 12:29-31

In my Father's house are many mansions: if it were not so, I would have told you. I go to prepare a place for you. And if I go and prepare a place for you, I will come again, and receive you unto myself; that where I am, there ye may be also.

John 14:2, 3

And yet I am not alone, because the Father is with me.

John 16:32

I appoint unto you a kingdom, as my Father hath appointed unto me; that ye may eat and drink at my table in my kingdom, and sit on thrones judging the twelve tribes of Israel.

Luke 22:29, 30

Whosoever drinketh of this water shall thirst again: but whosoever drinketh of the water that I shall give him shall never thirst; but the water that I shall give him shall be in him a well of water springing up into everlasting life.

John 4:13, 14

Jesus said unto them, I am the bread of life: he that cometh to me shall never hunger.

John 6:35

Repent: for the kingdom of heaven is at hand.

Matthew 4:17

Not every one that saith unto me, Lord, Lord, shall enter into the kingdom of heaven; but he that doeth the will of my Father which is in heaven.

Matthew 7:21

To him that overcometh will I give to eat of the hidden manna, and will give him a white stone, and in the stone a new name written, which no man knoweth saving he that receiveth it.

Revelation 2:17

He that overcometh, the same shall be clothed in white raiment; and I will not blot out his name out of the book of life, but I will confess his name before my Father, and before his angels.

Revelation 3:5

Verily, verily, I say unto you, That ye shall weep and lament, but the world shall rejoice; and ye shall be sorrowful, but your sorrow shall be turned into joy. A woman when she is in travail hath sorrow, because her hour is come: but as soon as she is delivered of the child, she remembereth no more the anguish, for joy that a man is born into the world. And ye now therefore have sorrow: but I will see you again, and your heart shall rejoice, and your joy no man taketh from you. And in that day ye shall ask me nothing. Verily, verily, I say unto you, Whatsoever ye shall ask the Father in my name, he will give it you. Hitherto have ye asked nothing in my name: ask, and ye shall receive, that your joy may be full.

John 16:20-24

To him that overcometh will I grant to sit with me in my throne, even as I also overcame, and am set down with my Father in his throne.

Revelation 3:21

Whosoever shall give you a cup of water to drink in my name, because ye belong to Christ, verily I say unto you, he shall not lose his reward.

Mark 9:41

LOVE

Love

A certain man went down from Jerusalem to Jericho, and fell among thieves, which stripped him of his raiment, and wounded him, and departed, leaving him half dead. And by chance there came down a certain priest that way; and when he saw him, he passed by on the other side. And likewise a Levite, when he was at the place, came and looked on him, and passed by on the other side. But a certain Samaritan, as he journeyed, came where he was; and when he saw him, he had compassion on him, and went to him, and bound up his wounds, pouring in oil and wine, and set him on his own beast, and brought him to an inn, and took care of him. And on the morrow when he departed, he took out two pence, and gave them to the host, and said unto him, Take care of him: and whatsoever thou spendest more, when I come again, I will repay thee. Which now of these three, thinkest thou, was neighbor unto him that fell among the thieves? And he said, He that showed mercy on him. Then said Jesus unto him, Go, and do thou likewise.

Luke 10:30-37
(Parable of the Good Samaritan)

Little children, yet a little while I am with you . . . .A new commandment I give unto you, That ye love one another; as I have loved you, that ye also love one another. By this shall all men know that ye are my disciples, if ye have love one to another.

John 13:33-35

Herein is my Father glorified, that ye bear much fruit; so shall ye be my disciples. As the Father hath loved me, so have I loved you: continue ye in my love. If ye keep my commandments, ye shall abide in my love; even as I have kept my Father's commandments, and abide in his love. These things have I spoken unto you, that my joy might remain in you, and that your joy might be full.

John 15:8-11

All things whatsoever ye would that men should do to you, do ye even so to them.

Matthew 7:12
(Sermon on the Mount)

If a kingdom be divided against itself, that kingdom cannot stand. And if a house be divided against itself, that house cannot stand.

Mark 3:24, 25

If a man love me, he will keep my words: and my Father will love him, and we will come unto him, and make our abode with him. He that loveth me not keepeth not my sayings: and the word which ye hear is not mine, but the Father's which sent me.

John 14:23, 24

Ye are my friend, if ye do whatsoever I command you. Henceforth I call you not servants; for the servant knoweth not what his lord doeth: but I have called you friends; for all things that I have heard of my Father I have made known unto you.

John 15:14, 15

He that hath my commandments, and keepeth them, he it is that loveth me: and he that loveth me shall be loved of my Father, and I will love him, and will manifest myself to him.

John 14:21

Blessed are they that hear the word of God, and keep it.

Luke 11:28

Blessed are the poor in spirit: for theirs is the kingdom of heaven.

Matthew 5:3
(Sermon on the Mount)

Blessed are they that mourn: for they shall be comforted.

Matthew 5:4
(Sermon on the Mount)

Blessed are the meek: for they shall inherit the earth.

Matthew 5:5
(Sermon on the Mount)

Blessed are they which do hunger and thirst after righteousness: for they shall be filled.

Matthew 5:6
(Sermon on the Mount)

Blessed are the merciful: for they shall obtain mercy.

Matthew 5:7
(Sermon on the Mount)

Blessed are the pure in heart: for they shall see God.

Matthew 5:8
(Sermon on the Mount)

Blessed are they which are persecuted for righteousness' sake: for theirs is the kingdom of heaven.

Matthew 5:10
(Sermon on the Mount)

Thou shalt love the Lord thy God with all thy heart, and with all thy soul, and with all thy mind. This is the first and great commandment. And the second is like unto it, Thou shalt love thy neighbor as thyself. On these two commandments hang all the law and the prophets.

Matthew 22:37-40

But I say unto you which hear, Love your enemies, do good to them which hate you, bless them that curse you, and pray for them which despitefully use you.

For if ye love them which love you, what thank have ye? for sinners also love those that love them. And if ye do good to them which do good to you, what thank have ye? for sinners also do even the same.

Be ye therefore merciful, as your Father also is merciful.

Luke 6:27, 28, 32, 33, 36

Love your enemies, bless them that curse you, do good to them that hate you, . . . that ye may be children of your Father which is in heaven: for he maketh his sun to rise on the evil and on the good, and sendeth rain on the just and on the unjust.

Be ye therefore perfect, even as your Father which is in heaven is perfect.

Matthew 5:44, 45, 48
(Sermon on the Mount)

PRAYING

Praying

The Pharisee stood and prayed thus with himself, God, I thank thee, that I am not as other men are, extortioners, unjust, adulterers, or even as this publican. I fast twice in the week, I give tithes of all that I possess. And the publican, standing afar off, would not lift up so much as his eyes unto heaven, but smote upon his breast, saying, God be merciful to me a sinner. I tell you, this man went down to his house justified rather than the other: for every one that exalteth himself shall be abased; and he that humbleth himself shall be exalted.

Luke 18:11-14

When ye pray, use not vain repetitions.

Matthew 6:7
(Sermon on the Mount)

And when thou prayest, thou shalt not be as the hypocrites are: for they love to pray standing in the synagogues and in the corners of the streets, that they may be seen of men. Verily I say unto you, They have their reward. But thou, when thou prayest, enter into thy closet, and when thou hast shut thy door, pray to thy Father which is in secret; and thy Father which seeth in secret shall reward thee openly.

Matthew 6:5, 6
(Sermon on the Mount)

And all things, whatsoever ye shall ask in prayer, believing, ye shall receive.

Matthew 21:22

When ye fast, be not, as the hypocrites, of a sad countenance: for they disfigure their faces, that they may appear unto men to fast. Verily I say unto you, They have their reward. But thou, when thou fastest, anoint thine head, and wash thy face; that thou appear not unto men to fast, but unto the Father which is in secret: and thy Father which seeth in secret shall reward thee openly.

Matthew 6:16-18
Sermon on the Mount)

There is nothing from without a man, that entering into him can defile him: but the things which come out of him, those are they that defile the man.

For from within, out of the heart of men, proceed evil thoughts, adulteries, fornications, murders, thefts, covetousness, wickedness, deceit, lasciviousness, an evil eye, blasphemy, pride, foolishness: all these evil things come from within, and defile the man.

Mark 7:15, 21-23

If ye abide in me, and my words abide in you, ye shall ask what ye will, and it shall be done unto you.

John 15:7

And he said unto them, When ye pray, say,
Our Father which art in heaven,
Hallowed be thy name.
Thy kingdom come.
Thy will be done,
as in heaven, so in earth.
Give us day by day our daily bread.
And forgive us our sins;
for we also forgive every one that is indebted to us.
And lead us not into temptation;
but deliver us from evil.

Luke 11:2-4

Your Father knoweth what things ye have need of, before ye ask him.

Matthew 6:8
(Sermon on the Mount)

If ye shall ask any thing in my name, I will do it.

John 14:14

Therefore I say unto you, What things soever ye desire, when ye pray, believe that ye receive them, and ye shall have them.

Mark 11:24

I say unto you, Ask, and it shall be given you; seek, and ye shall find; knock, and it shall be opened unto you. For every one that asketh receiveth; and he that seeketh findeth; and to him that knocketh it shall be opened.

Luke 11:9, 10

S

SERVICE

Service

Whosoever will come after me, let him deny himself, and take up his cross, and follow me. For whosoever will save his life shall lose it; but whosoever shall lose his life for my sake and the gospel's, the same shall save it. For what shall it profit a man, if he shall gain the whole world, and lose his own soul? Or what shall a man give in exchange for his soul?

Mark 8:34-37

O my Father, if it be possible, let this cup pass from me: nevertheless, not as I will, but as thou wilt.

Matthew 26:39

I am come that they might have life, and that they might have it more abundantly.

John 10:10

I am the good shepherd, and know my sheep, and am known of mine. As the Father knoweth me, even so know I the Father: and I lay down my life for the sheep.

John 10:14, 15

For whosoever shall do the will of my Father which is in heaven, the same is my brother, and sister, and mother.

Matthew 12:50

The Spirit of the Lord God is upon me; because the Lord hath anointed me to preach good tidings unto the meek; he hath sent me to bind up the broken-hearted, to proclaim liberty to the captives, and the opening of the prison to them that are bound; to proclaim the acceptable year of the Lord, and the day of vengeance of our God; to comfort all that mourn; to appoint unto them that mourn in Zion, to give unto them beauty for ashes, the oil of joy for mourning, the garment of praise for the spirit of heaviness.

Isaiah 61:1-3

Foxes have holes, and birds of the air have nests; but the Son of man hath not where to lay his head.

Luke 9:58

He that heareth you heareth me; and he that despiseth you despiseth me; and he that despiseth me despiseth him that sent me.

Luke 10:16

Ye shall be hated of all men for my name's sake: but he that endureth to the end shall be saved.

Matthew 10:22

For unto whomsoever much is given, of him shall be much required; and to whom men have committed much, of him they will ask the more.

Luke 12:48

He that receiveth you receiveth me; and he that receiveth me receiveth him that sent me.

And whosoever shall give to drink unto one of these little ones a cup of cold water only in the name of disciple, verily I say unto you, he shall in no wise lose his reward.

Matthew 10:40, 42

Go home to thy friends, and tell them how great things the Lord hath done for thee, and hath had compassion on thee.

Mark 5:19

Behold, I send you forth as sheep in the midst of wolves: be ye therefore wise as serpents, and harmless as doves.

Matthew 10:16

All power is given unto me in heaven and in earth. Go ye therefore, and teach all nations, baptizing them in the name of the Father, and of the Son, and of the Holy Ghost.

Matthew 28:18, 19

Be not afraid, but speak, and hold not thy peace: for I am with thee, and no man shall set on thee to hurt thee.

Acts 18:9, 10

Hearken; Behold, there went out a sower to sow.

And some fell among thorns, and the thorns grew up, and choked it, and it yielded no fruit. And other fell on good ground, and did yield fruit that sprang up and increased, and brought forth, some thirty, and some sixty, and some a hundred.

And these are they which are sown among thorns; such as hear the word, and the cares of this world, and the deceitfulness of riches, and the lusts of other things entering in, choke the word, and it becometh unfruitful. And these are they which are sown on good ground; such as hear the word, and receive it, and bring forth fruit, some thirty fold, some sixty, and some a hundred.

Mark 4:3, 7, 8, 18-20
(Parable of the Sower and the Seed)

If any man serve me, let him follow me; and where I am, there shall also my servant be: if any man serve me, him will my Father honor.

John 12:26

I tell you that, if these [disciples] should hold their peace, the stones would immediately cry out.

Luke 19:40

For where two or three are gathered together in my name, there am I in the midst of them.

Matthew 18:20

I will give you a mouth and wisdom, which all your adversaries shall not be able to gainsay nor resist.

Luke 21:15

If I then, your Lord and Master, have washed your feet; ye also ought to wash one another's feet.

John 13:14

When thou makest a dinner or a supper, call not thy friends, nor thy brethren, neither thy kinsmen, nor thy rich neighbors; lest they also bid thee again, and a recompense be made thee. But when thou makest a feast, call the poor, the maimed, the lame, the blind: and thou shalt be blessed; for they cannot recompense thee: for thou shalt be recompensed at the resurrection of the just.

Luke 14:12-14

Verily I say unto you, That this poor widow hath cast more in, than all they which have cast into the treasury: for all they did cast in of their abundance; but she of her want did cast in all that she had, even all her living.

Mark 12:43, 44

Woe unto you, scribes and Pharisees, hypocrites! for ye pay tithe of mint, and anise and cummin, and have omitted the weightier matters of the law, judgment, mercy and faith: these ought ye to have done, and not to leave the other undone. Ye blind guides, which strain at a gnat, and swallow a camel.

Matthew 23:23, 24

Take heed that ye do not your alms before men, to be seen of them: otherwise ye have no reward of your Father which is in heaven. Therefore when thou doest thine alms, do not sound a trumpet before thee, as the hypocrites do in the synagogues and in the streets, that they may have glory of men. Verily I say unto you, They have their reward. But when thou doest alms, let not thy left hand know what thy right hand doeth: that thine alms may be in secret: and thy Father which seeth in secret himself shall reward thee openly.

Matthew 6:1-4
(Sermon on the Mount)

Render therefore unto Caesar the things which are Caesar's; and unto God the things that are God's.

Matthew 22:21

No man can serve two masters: for either he will hate the one, and love the other; or else he will hold to the one, and despise the other. Ye cannot serve God and mammon.

Matthew 6:24
(Sermon on the Mount)

Freely ye have received, freely give.

Matthew 10:8

Ye are the light of the world. A city that is set on a hill cannot be hid. Neither do men light a candle, and put it under a bushel, but on a candlestick; and it giveth light unto all that are in the house. Let your light so shine before men, that they may see your good works, and glorify your Father which is in heaven.

Matthew 5:14-16

My doctrine is not mine, but his that sent me. If any man will do his will, he shall know of the doctrine, whether it be of God, or whether I speak of myself.

John 7:16, 17

T

TEMPTATION

Temptation

Take heed to yourselves, lest at any time your hearts be overcharged with surfeiting, and drunkenness, and cares of this life, and so that day come upon you unawares.

Luke 21:34

Watch ye and pray, lest ye enter into temptation. The spirit truly is ready, but the flesh is weak.

Mark 14:38

Get thee behind me, Satan.

Matthew 16:23

I say unto you, Swear not at all.

Matthew 5:34
(Sermon on the Mount)

Fear not them which kill the body, but are not able to kill the soul: but rather fear him which is able to destroy both soul and body in hell.

Matthew 10:28

The ground of a certain rich man brought forth plentifully: and he thought within himself, saying, What shall I do, because I have no room where to bestow my fruits? And he said, This will I do: I will put down my barns, and build greater; and there will I bestow all my fruits and my goods. And I will say to my soul, Soul, thou hast much goods laid up for many years; take thine ease, eat, drink, and be merry. But God said unto him, Thou fool, this night thy soul shall be required of thee: then whosc shall those things be, which thou hast provided? So is he that layeth up treasure for himself, and is not rich toward God.

Luke 12:16-21

Out of the abundance of the heart the mouth speaketh. A good man out of the good treasure of the heart bringeth forth good things: and an evil man out of the evil treasure bringeth forth evil things.

Matthew 12:34, 35

Even so every good tree bringeth forth good fruit; but a corrupt tree bringeth forth evil fruit. A good tree cannot bring forth evil fruit, neither can a corrupt tree bring forth good fruit.

Matthew 7:17, 18
(Sermon on the Mount)

I say unto you, Whosoever committeth sin is the servant of sin.

John 8:34

Whoso shall offend one of these little ones which believe in me, it were better for him that a millstone were hanged about his neck, and that he were drowned in the depth of the sea. Woe unto the world because of offenses! for it must needs be that offenses come; but woe to that man by whom the offense cometh! Wherefore if thy hand or thy foot offend thee, cut them off, and cast them from thee: it is better for thee to enter into life halt or maimed, rather than having two hands or two feet to be cast into everlasting fire. And if thine eye offend thee, pluck it out, and cast it from thee: it is better for thee to enter into life with one eye, rather than having two eyes to be cast into hell fire.

Matthew 18:6-9

Take heed that no man deceive you. For many shall come in my name, saying, I am Christ; and shall deceive many. And ye shall hear of wars and rumors of wars: see that ye be not troubled: for all these things must come to pass, but the end is not yet. For nation shall rise against nation, and kingdom against kingdom: and there shall be famines, and pestilences, and earthquakes, in divers places. All these are the beginning of sorrows.

Matthew 24:4-8

And then shall many be offended, and shall betray one another, and shall hate one another. And many false prophets shall rise, and shall deceive many. And because iniquity shall abound, the love of many shall wax cold. But he that shall endure unto the end, the same shall be saved.

Matthew 24:10-13.

Because thou hast kept the word of my patience, I also will keep thee from the hour of temptation, which shall come upon all the world, to try them that dwell upon the earth.

Revelation 3:10

I am the way, the truth, and the life: no man cometh unto the Father, but by me.

John 14:6

My grace is sufficient for thee: for my strength is made perfect in weakness.

2 Corinthians 12:9

And this gospel of the kingdom shall be preached in all the world for a witness unto all nations; and then shall the end come.

Matthew 24:14